BE THOU MY GUIDE
A BIBLE STUDY ON TRUSTING GOD

Margo Heath-Dupre

CONCORDIA PUBLISHING HOUSE • SAINT LOUIS

Published by Concordia Publishing House
3558 S. Jefferson Ave., St. Louis, MO 63118-3968
1-800-325-3040 • cph.org

Manufactured in the United States of America

1 2 3 4 5 6 7 8 9 10   29 28 27 26 25 24 23 22 21 20

DEDICATED

If time could tell,
The daylight would not fade
into the shadows of memories;
my soul would cry to pray.

If time could tell,
Oh, how my heart would bleed
for just a few more years
with my mother holding me.

If time could tell,
Perhaps the choices that were made
would yield a second look
At what the path had laid.

If time could tell,
A love shared with so much care,
to know a mother's precious love
is always, always there.

But time has told;
Two hearts that once beat as one,
will always be together in the
love of the Holy One.

*For Mom,
from your loving daughter Margo*

While life's dark maze I tread
And griefs around me spread,
        Be Thou my guide;
Bid darkness turn to day,
Wipe sorrow's tears away,
Nor let me ever stray
        From Thee aside.

Ray Palmer, "My Faith Looks Up to Thee" (public domain; *Lutheran Service Book* 702:3)

TABLE OF CONTENTS

ACKNOWLEDGMENTS

This study depended upon the help, advice, and encouragement of many. To those persons named and unnamed, I express my deepest gratitude. Specifically, I thank the following people for their collective involvement in developing *Be Thou My Guide*:

Christian Mentors:

My mother, Alma Jean Wasson Heath

My grandmothers, Annie Mae Johnson Heath and Mollie Ramsey Wasson

Their prayers lifted me, carried me, and allowed me to be the receiver of many blessings from God. On the laps, within the arms, at the kitchen tables, and on the church pews with these ladies, I grew to know and love the Lord.

Morale Boosters:

My loving husband, Rev. Brian C. Dupre

Our children, Antoine, Biancia, Marissa, and Martina

Within this gift of family, we continue to support one another in our faith journey to practice Christian diligence. I am truly thankful that through each individual and the collective experience of maturing as people of God, I have learned how to love the way God wants me to love.

Biblical Scripture Advisors:

Rev. James W. Turner, retired pastor: my first supporter at the inception of this study, he allowed me to introduce it at its infancy to the adult Bible study members of Holy Cross Lutheran Church (LCMS) in Detroit, Michigan. Furthermore, he has blessed me with his continued support as the study has evolved over the years.

Rev. Robert M. Roegner, Peace Lutheran Church (LCMS) in O'Fallon, Missouri, and senior doctrinal counselor for the Lutheran Women's

Missionary League from 2015 to 2017 (St. Louis, Missouri): I was blessed with Pastor Roegner's willingness to provide his counsel for doctrinal review and for the first blind review during the early stages of drafting the manuscript of this Bible study.

Biblical Scripture Consultant and Text Editor:

Rev. Brian C. Dupre, pastor and husband, Shadow of the Cross Lutheran Church (LCMS), Farmington Hills, Michigan: I am so very thankful to have had throughout all these years his willingness to find time, after completing his own sermons and writings, to assure that my understanding of Scripture was correct by clarifying meaning, reviewing structure of the overall study for clear understanding, and participating as a wordsmith when needed.

Special Interest Advisors:

The late Rev. Dr. Robert H. King, fourth vice president of The Lutheran Church—Missouri Synod, and a published author

Mrs. Jean King, EdD, adjunct instructor at Webster University

First and foremost, I offer my appreciation for their friendship and encouragement and also for their role as church leaders. Their support during our family's time at Concordia Seminary in St. Louis, as contributors to my husband's ministerial training (as a recipient of the Robert H. King Minority Student Endowment Fund) was truly a blessing. Our family regularly met with them for dinner and discussed the blessings of serving in the ministry. After seminary, Mrs. King and I continued to correspond until after Dr. King's death in 2016. Not only did they support my husband's ministry, but they also blessed me with their early support of my desire to write this study. Their willingness to read the basic concept and assess my writing and the value of the subject to Christian education was of great benefit. I am eternally grateful to have known them both.

Mrs. Zenarr A. Dishmon, MA in Teaching, National Board Certification for Teachers: I appreciate her willingness to participate as the Bible study facilitator test pilot and to provide insight that made the study easier to understand and practical for participants to apply. Without this valuable information, researching the real-life impact of the study would not have been possible.

USING THIS STUDY

Be Thou My Guide: A Bible Study on Trusting God can be used for individual or group study. Using this workbook for individual study offers the opportunity to better understand your current relationship with God mediated by the external Word (the Bible) and Sacrament. The personal-response questions are intentionally written to help you work at your own pace to help you engage in deeper thought and make personal connections to God.

Using *Be Thou My Guide* in a group not only allows for personal growth but also offers the added benefit of deepening fellowship and friendship. In a group study, one person may lead the entire course, or group members can take turns leading sessions. The leader(s) should coordinate with the group so all participants are aware of their responsibilities to the study of God's Word and to share and be mentored by one another.

Since this course deals with personal challenges, it is very important that participants get to know one another. Allow time so participants can express what they would like to gain from the study. Give them an opportunity to tell their names and share a little about their interest with this study; that is, where they are now in their relationship to God and where they would like to be in that relationship. Would they like to know God better or feel more confident in communicating with Him? The group leader may choose to share about herself first to guide the tone of this activity. Remind participants that this is a very personal growth process and all private issues shared during these sessions should remain within the group.

Pray for one another. Consider praying in a circle so all participants will feel equally involved. Invite them to pray for themselves, for one another, and as intercessors on behalf of loved ones. You may choose to take a few moments to listen to any desires, concerns, or issues, and then allow participants to pray for one another to close the session.

A WORD OF ENCOURAGEMENT FOR LEADERS

Pray for the Lord's guidance, and review each session before you lead the group. Depend on the Holy Spirit to guide your efforts to grow in this opportunity to practice discipleship. We are called to provide encouragement continuously through fellowship and prayer for one another. The apostle Paul says, "Let the word of Christ dwell in you richly, teaching and admonishing one another . . . with thankfulness in your hearts to God" (Colossians 3:16). *Admonish* here means to counsel or advise rather than to scold.

TIPS FOR LEADERS

Please read this workbook in full and then review the material prior to each session so that you are familiar with the concept of Christian diligence in general and the goal of each chapter in particular. Participants can read the chapters in advance so they can attend sessions with prepared questions and comments. Or they may take turns during the session to read sections of the study, then choose group discussion instead of writing individual answers. The Reading Group Discussion Guide in the back of the book (p. 106) is provided to help you facilitate discussion. Please remember that portions of the study will require participants to do some self-reflection.

As you begin each session, open with a prayer, then ask a participant to read aloud the purpose of the session and the objectives.

Throughout each session, ask for volunteers to read various Scripture passages that your group will study.

Give participants time to take notes, ask questions, and respond to the questions.

Encourage the participants to respond to one another. As the group leader, encourage participants to work together in a way that meets the needs of the whole group.

Close each session with prayer.

INTRODUCTION

THE IMPORTANCE OF SEEKING GOD'S WISDOM

In John 5:30, Jesus says, "I can do nothing on My own. As I hear, I judge, and My judgment is just, because I seek not My own will but the will of Him who sent Me."

Jesus makes it clear in His own words to us that He is not acting independently of our heavenly Father. He tells us that in everything and in every way, God's will is at work through Him. In this verse, our Savior is sharing with us the type of relationship He has with God. He is clearly telling us that He is willing to be submissive to the purposes of the almighty Father.

Likewise, we seek not our own will, but God's. In 1 Corinthians 1:30–31, the apostle Paul tells us, "You are in Christ Jesus, who became to us wisdom from God, . . . so that, as it is written, 'Let the one who boasts, boast in the Lord.'" Jesus is the Word of God (see John 1:1; 1:14), making Him the wisdom of God in the flesh (see 1 Corinthians 1:24). "In Him we have obtained an inheritance, having been predestined according to the purpose of Him who works all things according to the counsel of His will" (Ephesians 1:11). In our relationship with Jesus, we receive the wisdom of God (see 1 Corinthians 1:18–30). As we study the teachings of Jesus, the wisdom of God is spiritually poured out to us.

In James 3:17, we read, "The wisdom from above is first pure, then peaceable, gentle, open to reason, full of mercy and good fruits, impartial and sincere." When we seek God's wisdom, we can be in communion with His plan of salvation for us. But we cannot use our human abilities to perceive God's ways or understanding. Rather, the Holy Spirit works faith in our hearts to seek God's wisdom and His promise of salvation to us. God wants us to trust His guidance in His Word and believe it out of love for Him. As believers, we know that free will is given to us by our Creator; by His design, we have the freedom to make choices in our lives.

Most of us understand that we have the freedom to make choices about everything pertaining to our individual lives. As we grow into adulthood, that freedom increases as a type of right that we want to exercise. Yet we sometimes act or speak thoughtlessly due to a lack of emotional maturity, disrespect for one another, or inability to recognize our personal responsibility in various situations. Sometimes this free will allows us to create chaos in our own lives, in the lives of our loved ones, and in our communities. For some of us, this personal freedom becomes a habitual behavior that over time results in a callous shell around our hearts and souls.

In Romans 2:15, Paul tells us, "The work of the law is written on their hearts, while their conscience also bears witness, and their conflicting thoughts accuse or even excuse them." Our conscience will cause us to feel shame and guilt. God has written on every person's heart the Ten Commandments, which make us aware of our actions. He gives all of us the ability to know what is right and wrong. When we make excuses for our actions and attitude, we separate ourselves from God. When we separate from God, we follow the ways of the world, trusting in ourselves instead of seeking God's ways and trusting in Him. We begin to believe the image we create for social media platforms, community profiles, and public image. In 1 John 2:15–16, we read, "Do not love the world or the things in the world. . . .For all that is in the world—the desires of the flesh and the desires of the eyes and pride of life—is not from the Father." Not only will we begin to experience separation from God, but our actions also may cause others to believe that there are no consequences for our sin.

Yet there are consequences. Some are very real ones that show themselves painfully, slowly over time causing what can seem like irreparable damage to personal relationships; others come immediately with public ridicule that can overwhelm us. We experience these consequences as separation; emotional or physical distance; loss of jobs, friendships, family, or community membership; and deteriorating self-respect. The free will of making sinful choices affects our relationships with one another, but more importantly, it affects our relationship with God. We consider our choices with this understanding: "Train yourself for godliness; . . . godliness is of value in every way, as it holds promise for the present life and also for the life to come" (1 Timothy 4:7–8).

God's first lesson in free will regarding the choice to follow His spiritual instruction happens at the beginning of creation. God gave Adam and Eve the ability to make choices. He intentionally created us (male and female) in His image, formed Adam from dust, and breathed life into him (Genesis 1:27; 2:7) so we could have a spiritual relationship with Him. God provided Adam and Eve with all they needed. Yet the act of sin, born from their desire to be more like God and know good and evil, created a barrier between them and their Creator. In the Garden of Eden, we see the behavior of disobedience to God's instruction resulting in separation: an emotional, mental, spiritual, and physical distance between God and humankind. The sense of loss, separation, barrier, or distance we feel as a result of our choices in our relationships with one another is also realized in our relationship with God.

Yet in response to this act of disobedience, God works salvation. He rescued Adam and Eve, and us, from eternal damnation in an act of His grace. God did not create us to be puppets or robots with a predestined life in which our choices are without consequence in our own lives or the lives of others. God delights in our uniqueness and our creativity, just as we delight in the uniqueness of our family members and friends. He wants us to desire a relationship with Him and to want to obey His divine instruction for our lives. He wants us to understand that without His instruction, our lives will be filled with chaos, confusion, fear, and uncertainty. We will be consumed with impulse-control issues in our thoughts, words, and deeds. All are rooted in sin. When we put ourselves and others before Him by behaving with lack of faith, arrogance, pride, and idolatry, then we experience separation from God in consequence. Certainly, we are free to choose to obey or disobey, but we must realize that once we have made our choice, the consequences of that choice are not under our control. We cannot control what will happen as a result. The choice dictates the consequences—here on earth and in eternity.

God's wisdom is the foundation for living a Christian life. "His divine power has granted to us all things that pertain to life and godliness, through the knowledge of Him . . . so that . . . you may become partakers of the divine nature, having escaped from the corruption that is in the world because of sinful desire" (2 Peter 1:3–4). With the help of the Holy Spirit, we are able to hold onto our faith, which gives us knowledge of how to conduct ourselves and assures us that it is God who receives the glory. "For this very reason, make every effort to supplement your faith with virtue, and virtue with knowledge, and knowledge with self-control, and self-control with steadfastness, and steadfastness with godliness, and godliness with brotherly affection, and brotherly affection with love. For if these qualities are yours and are increasing, they keep you from being ineffective or unfruitful in the knowledge of our Lord Jesus Christ" (2 Peter 1:5–8). There is no other way for us to understand how He wants us to live and be in relationship with Him and one another. "For if you practice these qualities you will never fall" (2 Peter 1:10).

How can we develop intimate knowledge of these practices? "Continue in what you have learned and have firmly believed, knowing from whom you learned it and how . . . you have been acquainted with the sacred writings, which are able to make you wise for salvation through faith in Christ Jesus. All Scripture is breathed out by God and profitable for teaching . . . and for training" (2 Timothy 3:14–16).

When we seek God's wisdom, we receive His instruction and counsel. We study the Bible so that we can understand the character of God and learn how to relate to Him and to one another. Wisdom provides divine discipline that is critical to reflecting on our actions and words. It reminds us who we are as followers of Jesus. It protects us from the consequences of impulsive behaviors that are a natural state of our sinful being. Specifically, what do we gain by acting from the wisdom God grants? We gain the blessings of inner peace and self-esteem that come only from God, and we avoid the shame and guilt experienced when we act impulsively (Proverbs 3:13–18). Admittedly, gaining this discipline is easier said than done, because it requires practicing Christian diligence.

Christian diligence is an intentional mindset and purposeful behavior that Christians willingly embrace because we trust in God's love for us and because we want to draw closer to Him.

God offers us the gift of His Word, written and collected into the books of the Bible. His primary purpose in it is to create faith in our Savior, Jesus. His Word also reveals the Holy Trinity to us and teaches us how we can have a relationship with Him and with others. As believers, we understand the Holy Trinity to be the three persons of God. The First Person is God the Father, maker of all things in heaven and earth. The Second Person is Jesus

Christ, Son of the Father and our Redeemer, who offers us the unearned gift of salvation from the eternal damnation due to our sin. The Third Person is the Holy Spirit, sent by Jesus from God the Father, who intercedes for us with the Father, ministers to us, and bring us to faith.

To help us maintain clarity of what we believe, it is important to know the Christian statement of faith. The Nicene Creed provides us with a clear description of each of the three persons: God, the Father; Jesus, the Son and our Redeemer; and the Holy Spirit. The Nicene Creed is written in three sections that describe what we believe about each person of the Holy Trinity. When we say the Nicene Creed, we are purposely reminding ourselves of the specific differences in the purpose of each person of God. The sections of the Creed are intentionally taken from Scripture. Each section starts with "I believe" as a means to focus us on the truths of our life as Christians. "If you confess with your mouth that Jesus is Lord and believe in your heart that God raised Him from the dead, you will be saved. For with the heart one believes and is justified, and with the mouth one confesses and is saved" (Romans 10:9–10). The Creed continues by describing God as "the Father Almighty, maker of heaven and earth and of all things visible and invisible." As the maker, "God blessed the seventh day and made it holy, because on it God rested from all His work that He had done in creation" (Genesis 2:3). In the Book of Genesis, we learn that nothing existed before God. His creation of the world was completed in six days: declaring, speaking it into existence, organizing an operational and logical system that includes the order of day and night, and filling His creation with good things.

In the middle portion of our Christian statement of faith, we focus on God's promise of salvation by identifying who Jesus is and what He does for us. God announces this promise to sinful humankind and to the evil one: "I will put enmity between you and the woman, and between your offspring and her offspring; He shall bruise your head, and you shall bruise His heel" (Genesis 3:15). We consciously confess our belief that Jesus was conceived by the Holy Spirit of the Virgin Mary. We remind ourselves that He suffered by taking our punishment for the sins that we have done and will do during our life on earth. "Now is the judgment of this world; now will the ruler of this world be cast out. And I, when I am lifted up from the earth, will draw all people to Myself" (John 12:31–32). We proclaim that

He descended into hell after His death on the cross, that He rose on the third day, and that He ascended into heaven. "I came from the Father and have come into the world, and now I am leaving the world and going to the Father" (John 16:28). We are assured in our belief that He is alive today and sits at the right hand of the Father. We look forward to His coming again to earth "to judge both the living and the dead." "For this purpose I was born and for this purpose I have come into the world—to bear witness to the truth. Everyone who is of the truth listens to My voice" (John 18:37). We believe that He is our gift of redemption, offered to us by our heavenly Father because of His love for us.

The final portion of the Nicene Creed is a reminder that we cannot by ourselves come to faith in Jesus' gift of redemption. "When the Spirit of truth comes, He will guide you into all the truth, for He will not speak on His own authority, but whatever He hears He will speak, and He will declare to you the things that are to come" (John 16:13). Only with the Holy Spirit can we come to faith. Through the work of the Holy Spirit here on earth with us, we are sanctified, or marked holy. Before Jesus ascended into heaven, He promised us a helper and a comforter: "I will ask the Father, and He will give you another Helper, to be with you forever" (John 14:16). The Holy Spirit administers the Gospel to us through the Means of Grace—God's Holy Word and the Sacraments that Jesus instituted. We cannot discover it or seek it out on our own. And the Spirit comes to us only by these means, no others.

Scripture was given to us by God the Father. Scripture is comprised of Law and Gospel; both aim us toward salvation. The difference between Law and Gospel is that because of sin we cannot keep the Law. Moses was given the Law in the form of the Ten Commandments (Exodus 20:1–21). These laws are divided into two sections and establish for us the type of relationship we are to have with God and with one another. The first portion (the First through Third Commandments), what is referred to as the First Table of the Law, focuses us on how we are to relate to God. The second portion (the Fourth through Tenth Commandments, or the Second Table of the Law) tells us how to relate to one another.

God understands that we are not able to keep the Law. This is why He granted us unearned mercy and sent His beloved Son to earth. Jesus can and did keep the Law. "Do not think that I have come to abolish the Law or the

Prophets; I have not come to abolish them but to fulfill them" (Matthew 5:17).

Our Redeemer, Christ Jesus, came to fulfill the Law for our sake. He guarantees God's blessing and mercy toward us. As a gift of mercy, God the Father offered His Son, Jesus Christ, who is the sacrifice for the atonement of our sin. "A voice from heaven said, 'This is My beloved Son, with whom I am well pleased'" (Matthew 3:17). Jesus is our personal Savior. He came to each of us so we could receive the Good News, the Gospel. The Gospel is God's grace for us; it gives us a limited ability to fulfill the Law, because we remain both sinner and saint. As His children, we want to please Him, so we try to obey His commandments. However, our ability is limited because we are sinners; we have inherited our sinful flesh from Adam. At the same time, we are saints, because through Christ we have inherited eternal salvation and the unearned gift of grace. Through our relationship with Jesus as our personal Savior, we inherit the grace and mercy of the Father. Jesus invites us to receive His gift of salvation and forgiveness in the Sacraments of Holy Baptism and the Lord's Supper.

The Bible also provides us with the opportunity to study the personal relationships God the Father and God the Son had with people just like us. These men and women of the Bible are our Christian mentors. As we intimately learn their personal plights, we put that knowledge into the context of our own lives and mature spiritually as receivers of God's promises of goodness and mercy. These stories from God's Word help us find practical ways to build up our faith in times of trouble and to retain joy in knowing God's love. As we study His Word and grow in our faith, we are reminded that God's promise of peace and forgiveness remains forever true: "Therefore, while the promise of entering His rest still stands, let us fear lest any of you should seem to have failed to reach it" (Hebrews 4:1).

When we try to understand circumstances using only our human abilities, we easily become distracted. The distractions result from our human frailty, our sin, and Satan, who is always working to turn us away from God. We are tempted in many ways to develop trust in things of the world, not because we set out to behave this way, but because we are weak. Our senses are overwhelmed by enticements, stress of circumstances, empty promises, and in many cases, a false perception of security offered by those around us and by our own efforts. This is when we remember the promises of God. Some of us stray when things are going well, while others stray when difficulties arise. God is there in all situations and wants us to stay diligent toward Him in attitude, behavior, and prayer.

The Book of Hebrews tells us it is critical that we have faith. All that Jesus offers to us believers comes by faith. It does not come from witnessing miracles or experiencing horrific challenges; rather, it comes from hearing the Word of God. Hebrews 11:1 tells us that "faith is the assurance of things hoped for, the conviction of things not seen"; the chapter goes on to list people of great faith as concrete examples for how to live.

This study is designed to help clarify the process of Christian diligence so we may embrace the attitude and behavior necessary to fully recognize ourselves as living temples and testimonies to His goodness and grace. "Present your bodies as a living sacrifice, holy and acceptable to God, which is your spiritual worship. Do not be conformed to this world, but be transformed by the renewal of your mind, that by testing you may discern what is the will of God, what is good and acceptable and perfect" (Romans 12:1–2).

We can be encouraged because Jesus understands all our weaknesses. Born as a man living among us, He was tempted in every way. Rest assured that He can help us with every challenge. "Therefore, since we have been justified by faith, we have peace with God through our Lord Jesus Christ" (Roman 5:1). Throughout the Christian life in both ancient and current times, we will experience suffering. In 1 Peter 4:7, we are told that this world will soon come to an end. This end could come at any time. Peter tells us to be mindful of our behavior and attitudes by staying focused on God through prayer and by living as examples of Christian love (1 Peter 4:8–11). In other words, Peter is urging us to practice Christian diligence.

It is difficult to practice Christian diligence because it involves discipline. "See to it that no one takes you captive by philosophy and empty deceit, according to human tradition, according to the elemental spirits of the world, and not according to Christ" (Colossians 2:8). When we are mindful of God's Word, we are more attentive to our relationship with Him. We do this through studying the Bible, prayer, worship, and participating in the Holy Sacraments of Baptism and the Lord's Supper. We will dive into our discussion on prayer later. Here, we will expand on Bible study, worship, and the Holy Sacraments.

The Holy Bible is the true Word of God, Scripture that teaches us all we need to know about Him. Dedicating our time to learning about God in Bible class helps us to self-correct and lovingly guide one another. "For the

LORD gives wisdom; from His mouth come knowledge and understanding" (Proverbs 2:6). Knowledge of His Law (the Commandments) leads us to understand our sin; the Law is a mirror, showing us our guilt and convicting us. Under the Law, we have no hope and no recourse. Remember, though, that the primary purpose of the Bible is not to condemn us but to work faith in our hearts. We learn about the Son of God, Jesus Christ, and His work of salvation by hearing the Gospel proclaimed in the divine service and by reading the Bible. When we come to know about God's love for us in Jesus, it makes us want to repent of our sin, to learn more about Him and His ways, and to share our faith in His grace with others.

God wants to know that we are willing to acknowledge all He does for us. One way we do this is to dedicate time just for Him. We should want to worship God because it is our opportunity to show reverence, give thanks, praise, confess and repent, receive Him in the Sacraments, petition Him in prayer, and gather with other believers. In worship, we come to God and focus only on Him. During this time, we are not only thanking Him for all He has done for us and will do for us but we are also acknowledging Him for who He is—our everything. We are humbling ourselves before His altar and acknowledging Him as the one true living God.

God provides us with the blessings of Holy Baptism. Baptism was instituted by Christ: "as Christ loved the church and gave Himself up for her, that He might sanctify her, having cleansed her by the washing of water with the Word, so that He might present the church to Himself in splendor, without spot or wrinkle or any such thing, that she might be holy and without blemish" (Ephesians 5:25–27). Baptism forgives our sins, rescues us from the devil, and gives us eternal salvation. Jesus said, "All authority in heaven and on earth has been given to Me. Go therefore and make disciples of all nations, baptizing them in the name of the Father and of the Son and of the Holy Spirit, teaching them to observe all that I have commanded you. And behold, I am with you always, to the end of the age" (Matthew 28:18–20).

It is not simply the water but the Word of God and His command together that allow us to receive the blessings of Baptism. This holy gift of new spiritual life provides us with an intentional behavioral opportunity to participate in fellowship with God. Through Baptism, we receive the gift of forgiveness and eternal salvation through our relationship with His begotten Son.

The Lord's Supper is the other Sacrament instituted by God the Son: "He took bread, . . . and gave it to them, saying, 'This is My body, which is given for you.' . . . Likewise the cup after they had eaten, saying, 'This cup that is poured out for you is the new covenant in My blood'" (Luke 22:19–20). Jesus tells us that the Sacrament of His body and blood brings us forgiveness. He tells us plainly that this act of receiving the Lord's Supper gives us access to His gift of forgiveness. Therefore, we want to practice this behavior as faithful followers of Jesus. It is not simply the bread and wine but the Word of God and His command together that do the work of allowing us to receive the blessings of forgiveness, life, and salvation. Martin Luther called it "the food of souls."

To live as people of God means to be in a relationship with God in His Word and in the Sacraments. The wisdom we gain through our relationship with Him will not make our lives easier in the way the world would have us expect. Rather, the wisdom gained in knowing who Jesus is and what He is doing for us provides us with the comfort of knowing that whatever challenges we face in life, we are not alone. In addition, we can be comforted knowing that He has won victory over sin, death, and the devil for us so that we can look forward to life in eternity with Him.

What intentional behaviors should we willingly embrace because we love God?

We willingly embrace these intentional behaviors throughout our lives to show respect for our relationship with God because we love Him:

- Giving glory to God
- Studying His Word
- Praying
- Confessing our sins and repenting of them
- Participating in the Divine Service
- Remembering our Baptism
- Receiving the Lord's Supper
- Showing love for others so they can know His love through us

If we refrain from these behaviors, do we truly love God? A better question may be this: if we really love God and want a relationship with Him, why would we reject these behaviors? These behaviors are how we respond to Him.

What has Jesus left on earth to guide us in our effort to be diligent to the will of God?

In a word: Scripture. The apostle Paul wrote, "All Scripture is breathed out by God and profitable for teaching, for reproof, for correction, and for training in righteousness, that the man of God may be complete, equipped for every good work" (2 Timothy 3:16–17). In addition, Jesus asks the Father to provide the Holy Spirit to help us live a life that allows God to work His will among His children. Jesus tells us, "The Holy Spirit, whom the Father will send in My name, He will teach you all things and bring to your remembrance all that I have said to you" (John 14:26). Jesus speaks these words to us as believers. This is the Spirit of truth, who knows both the Father and the Son; He will speak truth to us.

How do we stay connected to Jesus with the help of the Holy Spirit?

We stay connected to the Holy Spirit by studying the Word of God and by receiving the Lord's Supper. Jesus sent the Holy Spirit to guide and protect us while we live here on earth. We stay connected to the Spirit of truth through worship, prayer, and Bible study; the Holy Spirit helps us recognize the message of Jesus and receive it as His holy direction. Hearing God's Word is the beginning of having a relationship with Him. The more we study the Bible and learn of God's love for us, the more we want to know Him and the more we learn how He seeks us out and shows His grace to us. Exploring the effort He makes to love and protect us makes us want to stay close to Him. Staying close to Him strengthens us in our effort to resist the temptations and distortions that are in the world and from Satan.

How are we to communicate to God?

Jesus gives us specific instruction on how to pray when we want to be alone with the Lord. He tells us what mindset to have, what to do, and how to speak:

- When we pray, we should go to a private room, shut the door, and pray to our heavenly Father; He will hear us in secret and reward us openly (see Matthew 6:6).
- We should not use meaningless repetition of words, thinking that many words are needed. Our Father in heaven already knows what our needs are before we ask (see Matthew 6:7–8).

Jesus' instructions tell us to be intentional in three ways:

- Behavior—be in a quiet place, without interruptions; set aside time for us and God.
- Attitude—don't use vain words in an attempt to impress God.
- Relationship—ask boldly in prayer, although He already knows our needs and will respond to us according to His will for us.

AN INTENTIONAL ATTITUDE OF JOY IN KNOWING GOD

In Philippians 4, Paul wrote to the Church at Philippi, encouraging them to be intentional about maintaining an attitude of joy in knowing our Lord. Furthermore, he shared with the congregation that he had learned through his tribulations and triumphs to be content. Paul wrote that his relationship with God allowed him to be content in all circumstances, whether he was facing plenty or was in need, experiencing hunger or abundance. He understood that God would provide all the strength necessary for him to endure any issues. Paul had intentionally chosen to have an attitude of contentment.

Christian diligence begins when we are aware of and choose to change our thinking. When we practice intentionality, we gain new understanding about our experiences in this world and our choice of responding to them. Our attitude is an intentional behavior that is within our human power to adjust and change. Christian intentionality involves everything we do, feel, and believe, starting with seeking God and choosing to spend time with Him through the study of His Word and in worship and choosing to receive Him in the Lord's Supper. As we study the Bible, we learn that God wants us to bring our cares to Him. Prayer is the behavior God provides to us for personally speaking to Him, expressing our repentance, fear, praise, requests, and thankfulness.

AN INTENTIONAL BEHAVIOR OF PRAYER TO SPEND TIME WITH JESUS

Prayer is an intentional behavior, practiced to communicate to God, that requires dedication and fervency. Jesus spent much time in prayer to the Father in heaven regarding His circumstances on earth and regarding other people. What is most important about Jesus' prayers? His prayers aligned with what He knew as the will of God. He had a constant relationship with God that included communing with Him in times and places set aside for just the two of them. In the Garden of Gethsemane, Jesus told His Father that His human side was fearful because His flesh had not experienced death. In Matthew 26:42, He prayed to God, saying, "My Father, if this cannot pass unless I drink it, Your will be done." In this situation, Jesus showed His humanity and proved that He understands when we are afraid of difficult events in our life. God invites us to go to Him in prayer and tell Him our fears. We need not allow fear to lead us to quit God's plan for us. Jesus continues in prayer, telling God that although His flesh is fearful, He will complete God's plan because He knows it must be done to atone for our sins. God knew that Jesus' flesh was fearful, and He also knew that Jesus would come to Him in prayer about it. God the Father provided Jesus the Son with the spiritual courage to fulfill His will. Jesus modeled spiritual courage in being diligent to accomplish God's plan for His life on earth, and He expressed boldly God's authority in His words and His actions. We learn from His prayer life, His deliberate words to the Father in heaven, that He was intentionally committed in attitude and behavior to follow God's will.

AN INTENTIONAL MINDSET OF PATIENCE TO WAIT FOR GOD'S DIVINE INSTRUCTION

We likewise can have an attitude of patience as we commune with God, knowing He listens, and we can trust Him to answer. Patience is a mindset that controls the impulses. When we choose patience, we are allowing God to identify His way for accomplishing His will for us. He is always on time and always has our best interest at heart. As His children, we can take comfort in knowing that everything that happens, or doesn't happen, is a part of His masterful plan.

In our prayer life, we can be intentionally submissive to the answers God is providing. Sometimes He says yes, and sometimes He says no. He tells us no when our request does not align with His plan for our lives. When we feel distant from God because of our deeds, desires, emotional pain, physical challenges, or mental anguish, we can seek Him out in prayer and study His Word for reassurance that His gift of the Holy Spirit will guide and help us to be pleasing in His sight. "And this is the confidence that we have toward Him, that if we ask anything according to His will He hears us. And if we know that He hears us in whatever we ask, we know that we have the requests that we have asked of Him" (1 John 5:14–15).

AN INTENTIONAL PERSONAL RELATIONSHIP WITH GOD MEDIATED BY THE EXTERNAL WORD AND SACRAMENT

Through intentional behaviors, we are able to grow closer to knowing Him and allowing Him into our lives to comfort, forgive, love, and guide. In this way, we become convinced that we have our own personal relationship with Him that is like no other. Unwavering faith in the one true living God, a prayer life, time in His Word, hearing the Gospel proclaimed, sincere repentance, receiving His body and blood at the Holy Table, and a thankful heart are what it takes to become convinced that God is real in our lives. As children of the heavenly Father, we continuously choose to be obedient to His teachings, commandments, guidance, and directives, in response to His love for us.

In the Book of James, we are reminded to stay disciplined in our behavior throughout any testing of our faith. In his first chapter, James explains that if we neglect to seek the wisdom of God, then the trials of life may destroy us through sinful behaviors. James clearly describes the consequences of this neglect, making clear that each of us is tempted by her own desires and not by God (vv. 12–15). Our heavenly Father tempts no one. Furthermore, James encourages us to study the Word of God and abide by it (vv. 19–27). As Christians, we want to model Christ in our responses: slow to speak, swift to hear, calm in our interactions, and active in reading the Word of God. When we do what has been implanted in us through studying the Bible, our actions keep us aligned with God. We must embrace our faith as a gift from God the Father, not from our own ability to do anything. Hebrews 4:15–16 tells us that we don't have a high priest who is unable to know our weaknesses. Rather, we have a High Priest who has been tempted just as we are but who never sinned; He allows us to come to the throne for mercy and grace. Studying His Word is our only way to assure that our thoughts align with His.

By reading the Scriptures, we are reminded of God's promises regarding His love, devotion, and power over all things of this world. Being in the Word helps us to hold onto our belief in God's ability and reminds us to be content in our present state. We can always depend on God to work in our lives to accomplish His will. We read in Philippians 2:13, "It is God who works in you, both to will and to work for His good pleasure." Therefore, let us continue to encourage one another to practice Christian diligence: "Keep hold of instruction; do not let go; guard her, for she is your life" (Proverbs 4:13).

PRAYER OF PREPARATION

Dear Lord, as I begin this study on Christian diligence, help me to grow closer to You as my healer, protector, helper, counselor, friend, and most of all, my Redeemer and Savior. Help me to hold onto my belief in You to work things out for my good during times of difficulty, and anchor me in faith to be content and patient, assured that Your provision is enough for me. Lord, I ask that You reveal to me the behaviors, attitudes, and mindset that are acceptable to You so I can better receive Your divine instruction through the study of Your Word and through the Sacrament, and be changed. In the name of Jesus, I pray. Amen.

THEME: BELIEVING IN GOD'S ABILITY

LAW/GOSPEL

"The LORD is near to the brokenhearted and saves the crushed in spirit."
(Psalm 34:18)

OBJECTIVE FOR SESSION 1

I will understand that I can depend on God's ability in any circumstances.

WHAT WILL I LEARN?

I will learn that during times of anxiousness and frustration, my faith in
God's ability need never be in doubt.

HOW WILL I LEARN THIS?

I will learn it through examining God's reaction to Moses when he
questioned God's ability.

PREPARATION FOR STUDY: RELATIONAL UNDERSTANDING

I will understand that I can depend on God's ability in any circumstances.

Staying mentally focused on Jesus—keeping our eyes on the cross and taking our burdens to the Lord—is not always the first thing we do in times of trouble. As human beings, we are rather easily distracted when things are going well. And when things are not going well, we may turn inward. Sometimes there is so much noise in our lives, it is almost impossible to think, let alone pray. At other times, we feel so much pain that we believe we cannot bear it any longer. It is during insurmountable times, when we feel weak and ineffective, that we focus on God and His ability to take care of us and those we love. We may endure times when there is no food in the refrigerator and no money in the house, no funds to pay for school books or shoes, no way we can see to get through to our next paycheck, make the mortgage payment, or simply pay for a field trip for our children. These situations most assuredly make us feel anxious or frustrated—if not outright panicked.

It is when we feel ourselves buckling under the stress that we can be assured that God is in full battle for us. Even so, He still wants to hear from us in prayer, and He wants us to acknowledge our need for Him.

PRAYER OF PREPARATION

Dear Lord, during times when I feel stressed and weighed down, burdened by difficulties and challenges, help me to remember that my solace is to turn to You. Help me keep in mind that everything is in Your mighty hands and comes under Your authority. Teach me to be thankful that no matter what happens, You provide what I need most—forgiveness of my sins and the promise of all good things in the life to come. I thank You, Lord, for continuing to remind me, just as You did Moses, that I can trust Your ability in all circumstances. In Jesus' name, I pray. Amen.

OUR MENTOR—MOSES

ABOUT THE TEXT

God called Moses to return to Egypt for His people and lead them to the Promised Land. Throughout the Israelites' experience in the wilderness, God dealt with all their obstacles. Nevertheless, the people complained as if they did not know God. Moses prayed to God and complained that the responsibility for the people was too great. He expressed frustration and anxiety, feeling dissatisfied with his ability to provide for them. This feeling of discontent caused Moses to address God with the same attitude of complaint as the people he was called to lead. He questioned God's ability. God forgave Moses and helped him, and He stayed with the people both day and night. But even though He provided for the people, God also disciplined them. This session teaches us that our relationship with God provides both forgiveness and discipline according to His will.

OUR MENTOR—MOSES

Scripture Reading: Numbers 11:4–25

1. What caused God to become angry and Moses to complain? See Numbers 11:4–15.

_____

_____

_____

_____

_____

_____

2. When have you complained to others about the way God has provided for you, using phrases such as "I know I can do better than this," or "Things aren't like they use to be"?

_____

_____

_____

_____

_____

_____

3. How did God respond to the complaining? See Numbers 11:16–20.

_____

_____

_____

_____

_____

_____

4. What did Moses say to God about the circumstances? See Numbers 11:21–22.

_____

_____

_____

_____

_____

_____

5. How did God respond to Moses? See Numbers 11:23–25.

_____

_____

_____

_____

_____

_____

6. Why do you think God responded to Moses in the way that He did?

_____

_____

_____

_____

_____

_____

SESSION CONCLUSION

In this session, God reminded Moses—and us—that we are to rely not on our ability but on His. Believers continuously remind one another of God's myriad of blessings, even when traveling together through a wilderness. Our relationship with God can be impacted by our bad attitudes, expressed to Him as complaining, whining, and a sense of entitlement, just as it was among the Israelites. We can displease God when we frustrate those whom God has provided to us as loved ones and caregivers. Even as we experience God's discipline, we can be sure that all of His gifts are good; therefore, we receive them with a joyful heart and praises of thanksgiving. We learn from Moses that we should never doubt God's ability to take care of us and that He will keep His promise in every circumstance. God reveals His character as a keeper of His promise to lead us to the promised land—eternal life with Him in heaven.

PRAYER STARTER

Dear Lord, there are times in my life when I complain and move away from You. I now understand that in my complaining, I am expressing my lack of faith. Help me to approach You in prayer with a repentant heart, always recognizing that Your gifts are best for me. In Jesus' name, I pray. Amen.

PRAYER PROMPT

"The friendship of the LORD is for those who fear Him, and He makes known to them His covenant." (Psalm 25:14)

THEME: REALIZING MY ACCOUNTABILITY TO GOD

LAW/GOSPEL

"I am not ashamed of the gospel, for it is the power of God for salvation to everyone who believes." (Romans 1:16)

OBJECTIVE FOR SESSION 2

I will understand that God's power is limitless.

WHAT WILL I LEARN?

I will learn that my accountability to God is to believe in His Word, ability, and promises with faith and courage.

HOW WILL I LEARN THIS?

I will learn this by studying how God established His relationship with Joshua after Moses' death.

PREPARATION FOR STUDY: RELATIONAL UNDERSTANDING

I will understand that God's power is limitless.

Sometimes God may inspire us to proclaim our faith in Him for something we are convicted to do, but we may hesitate. We may shy away from sharing our conviction because of fear that we won't speak correctly or won't be believed by family and friends. We may lack support for what others may label as a fantasy or an unobtainable goal. People may say they don't understand or don't see the benefit in what we are speaking about. Others may tell us to be quiet because they don't want to hear about it anymore or that it's a silly idea. It is perfectly all right for others not to understand the message, direction, or answer we get from God. God speaks to all of humanity in His Word, the Bible; however, through our personal study of Scripture, God is speaking directly to us. He is communing with us individually because His will for our life is personal; He placed us in this time and place and created us with vocations that we use to serve Him and benefit others. As brothers and sisters in Christ, we support and encourage one another to stay in prayer and believe in the answers that God is providing us in His Word. Not only does our Creator have a perfect will for us as individuals, but He also wills that all people draw near to Him and receive the gifts of faith, forgiveness, and everlasting life.

PRAYER OF PREPARATION

Dear Lord, thank You for reminding me of my accountability as a believer. Help me to learn that the relationship You established with Joshua is the same that You want with me. Thank You for Your patience as I mature in my understanding of who You are and how You guide my faith walk. With the help of the Holy Spirit, I know that I am not alone and I have what is needed to be courageous and faithful in Your ability and promises in every situation. In Jesus' name, I pray. Amen.

OUR MENTOR—JOSHUA

ABOUT THE TEXT

Joshua had been a servant of Moses, and although he had witnessed Moses' relationship with God, it was time to establish his own. God changed how Joshua thought in order to complete His preparation for accomplishing His will for Joshua's life. Through an interaction between Moses and Joshua, God gave Joshua the most important understanding that he would need about God's ability. God wanted Joshua to change his thinking so his thoughts and reactions would be as a man of God who understood His authority. This session lists the specific behaviors God requires of us to stay connected to Him in thought, word, and deed.

OUR MENTOR—JOSHUA

Scripture Reading: Numbers 11:26–29; 27:18–23; Joshua 1:1–10

1. What was the cause for Joshua's plea to Moses? See Numbers 11:26–28.

    _____

    _____

    _____

    _____

    _____

2. What do you think Moses meant when he asked Joshua, "Are you jealous for my sake?" See Numbers 11:29.

    _____

    _____

    _____

    _____

    _____

3. What was the importance of Moses' response to Joshua's plea?

    _____

    _____

    _____

    _____

    _____

4. What is the importance of understanding how God gives to others?

    _____

    _____

    _____

    _____

    _____

5. What did God direct Moses to do before the Israelites crossed the Jordan? See Numbers 27:18–23.

    _____

    _____

    _____

    _____

    _____

6. What was God's promise to Joshua? See Joshua 1:1–5.

    _____

    _____

    _____

    _____

    _____

7. What is happening in my life that I need to do as God said to Joshua, "Be strong and courageous"? See Joshua 1:6–7.

    _____

    _____

    _____

    _____

    _____

    _____

SESSION CONCLUSION

In this session, we learn that the principles of Christian diligence, through embracing intentional behaviors and attitude, were clearly taught to Joshua by God the Father in Joshua 1:1–10.

In our own Christian lives, we read the Bible, God's Holy Word, and believe it as truth and only truth. In other words, we do not entertain other resources that can affect our relationship with God. During and after reading this passage, think about its message according to your personal life (needs, desires, circumstances, and so on). Allow the Word of God to change your thoughts by what you learn (that is, align your thoughts with God's). Assess your behavior and attitude; will you behave obediently, waiting patiently for clear direction with full faith that God is with you in every moment? In our study of the life of Joshua, who was chosen specifically to care for and lead God's people into the Promised Land, we see that his humanity is the same as ours. God is speaking to us through Joshua.

PRAYER STARTER

Dear Lord, as I praise You, help me to remember who You are and to trust in You in every way. With the help of the Holy Spirit, increase my understanding of You through studying Your Word so I will complete Your plan for my life. Amen.

PRAYER PROMPT

"Fear God and keep His commandments, for this is the whole duty of man." (Ecclesiastes 12:13)

THEME: DISCOVERING GOD'S PATH FOR MY LIFE

LAW/GOSPEL

"Your word is a lamp to my feet and a light to my path." (Psalm 119:105)

OBJECTIVES FOR SESSION 3

I will seek God's wisdom through time in His Word, in the Divine Service, and in prayer.

I will understand the charge of authority given to the believer.

WHAT WILL I LEARN?

I will learn that I need the divine guidance of God in all I do.

HOW WILL I LEARN THIS?

I will explore how the authority God delegated to Solomon was misunderstood, neglected, abandoned, misused, and executed; this will help me to align my own behavior and attitude with God's desire to use me for His purposes.

PREPARATION FOR STUDY: RELATIONAL UNDERSTANDING

I will seek God's wisdom through time in His Word, in the Divine Service, and in prayer.

Solomon wasn't a perfect man, but he understood that God's path for his life would require wisdom. Only God could provide the wisdom for dealing with the challenges Solomon and his people would face. We embrace the attitude that Solomon had toward God by first going to Him in prayer, confessing our need for Him, and asking that He open our hearts and minds to hear His unique message for us. Solomon recognized that God had provided him with the gift of discerning situations and making judgments that were right for the people. He asked for God's help, and he received it because it was an unselfish request. Quiet your mind and read God's Word. Take time away from the world and allow your heart to connect with the Spirit of God. Spending time with God in His Word gives strength, peace, knowledge, and confidence to stand against persecution, affliction, worldly concerns, deceit, and social pressure. Just as Solomon went to God in prayer, asking for understanding for his new authority (1 Kings 3:7–12), so we also humbly petition God to prepare us to do His will and not our own.

I will understand the charge of authority given to the believer.

To assure that we start with the same understanding, let's look at the meaning of the word *authority*. Generally, *authority* means to have power to give orders and make decisions; to have control over someone or something. As Christians, we understand that all authority comes from God, who in turn gives us authority to "go therefore and make disciples of all nations, baptizing them in the name of the Father and of the Son and of the Holy Spirit, teaching them to observe all that I have commanded you" (Matthew 28:18–20). With the power of the Holy Spirit working in us, we can put off the old Adam and turn away from our sin (see 1 John 5:4–5).

But sometimes we struggle with this authority. We may misunderstand how to function under God's divine authority and within the earthly authority He entrusts to us. Our sinful nature causes us to rebel, reject, or abandon authority. Often, the struggle is due to a lack of direction from those who have authority over us. Sometimes the struggle is a result of how authority has been used for or against us at different times in our lives. As we mature in our understanding that authority is a gift from God and distributed to various persons, including ourselves, for His purposes, we can feel less vulnerable and more empowered in our experiences (see Luther's explanation of the Fourth Commandment in the Small Catechism). The sense of vulnerability is replaced with confidence through faith that God enables us to grow closer in relationship with Him and to grow resistant to the wiles of the devil. Authority requires us to develop the responsible behaviors of a righteous person through studying God's Word and recognizing our accountability to Him. God has distributed various types of human authority in four major areas:

- Parenting in the family
- Marriage in the home
- Work in employment
- Service in government

Take a moment to think about the authority God provides to you that draws you to Him and moves you to point others to know Him. Perhaps some of these vocations and roles have occurred to you: parent, work supervisor, teacher, professor, coach, team captain, pastor, committee chairperson, spouse, custodian, teacher, police officer, sibling, babysitter, uncle, aunt, foster parent, stepparent, school principal, delivery truck driver, mail carrier, scout leader, social worker, retail clerk, information technology technician, administrative assistant, and grandparent.

Are you starting to see the picture? It does not matter the length of time or the scope of the role because all vocations, roles, and jobs give us the responsibility to be about His business. As believers, we understand that whatever our role of authority is and for whatever amount of time we have it, we use it for God's purposes to provide others with the opportunity to know who He is, how much He cares for them, and what Jesus does for them. Throughout this study, you will find introspective questions to help you think about how God has drawn you closer to Him and, at the same time, given you opportunities to help others know Him.

PRAYER OF PREPARATION

Dear Lord, as I study to discover Your guidance in my life, help me to understand that any authority, great or small, is granted for Your purposes. With the help of the Holy Spirit, help me to stay clear of all things that will offend You. Please protect me from making decisions or rejecting responsibility based on my own understanding. Through study of Your

Word and through the proclamation of the Gospel in the Divine Service, guide me and keep me so that after I have discovered or confirmed Your path for my life, Your will is done. In Jesus' name, I pray. Amen.

OUR MENTOR—SOLOMON

ABOUT THE TEXT

Out of love for God, Solomon learned from his father, David, about the type of relationship to seek with God. As king, Solomon sought God in prayer for guidance to govern the Israelites. However, as husband and father, he neglected his authority, seeking a life of acceptance by others instead of by God. Solomon did not seek God's guidance on all matters, even those under human authority. This session teaches us that the wisdom of God permeates all areas of our Christian life.

OUR MENTOR—SOLOMON

Scripture Reading: 1 Kings 3:1–15; 9:1–9; 10:1–23; 11:1–10

1. What areas of human authority in Solomon's life directly impacted his relationship with God? See 1 Kings 3:1–15.

    _____

    _____

    _____

    _____

    _____

2. What caused Solomon to seek God's wisdom to govern?

    _____

    _____

    _____

    _____

    _____

3. What caused Solomon to neglect seeking God's wisdom to marry?

    _____

    _____

    _____

    _____

    _____

4. What was the importance of God making a second appearance to Solomon? See 1 Kings 9:1–9.

    _____

    _____

    _____

    _____

    _____

5. How did God show He was pleased with Solomon's prayer for wisdom? See 1 Kings 10:1–23.

_____

_____

_____

_____

_____

_____

6. How has the use of human authority, mine or someone else's, caused others to experience spiritual, emotional, or mental conflict?

_____

_____

_____

_____

_____

7. What was the sin of Solomon's relationship with others that caused irreparable harm to his relationship with God? See 1 Kings 11:1–10.

_____

_____

_____

_____

_____

_____

SESSION CONCLUSION

When we have God-given authority over others, whether our position is great or small, we are still under His authority and are held accountable to Him. It should be clearly noticeable to those entrusted to us that we are functioning as an instrument of God. Our understanding of our authority is revealed through our desire to be mindful of God's will through study of His Holy Word. We also express it in our behavior in church, home, work, and community. Through prayer (Psalm 86:7), we continually ask God for guidance from the Holy Spirit to help us keep His commandments and worship faithfully as a measure against all we do and say. Solomon's character flaws and virtues are no different from our own. God gave Solomon authority to govern the Israelites and the charge to build the temple for Him. Solomon understood God's expectations of him and asked for the spiritual gift of wisdom to make righteous judgments for people. Although Solomon discovered, embraced, and fulfilled God's will to build the temple and rule over the people using the gift of wisdom God bestowed on him, he stirred God's anger by listening to his idolatrous wives and turning from God. This resulted in God's anger coming down on the people.

In Exodus 20:2–17, God gave His people the Ten Commandments. As the son of King David, Solomon was taught these commandments, one of which was to worship only God. On his deathbed, King David reminded Solomon of the type of relationship he was to have with God: to obey His directions and laws, keep the Ten Commandments, and abide by the covenant God had made with the Israelites (1 Kings 2:1–4). Yet Solomon chose to abandon the covenant God made with the Israelites. Despite his wisdom, Solomon still fell into great sin. He did not abide by the covenant or teach his sons about God, and he did not seek God's guidance in the matter of marriage. The covenant is not only between God and the believers as a community but also between God and each individual for all time. Through spending time studying His Holy Word and receiving the Sacrament, we continue to be aware of our relationship with God and can abide by the covenant.

PRAYER STARTER

Dear Lord, I ask, in the name of Your dear Son, Jesus, for forgiveness during my time of weakness or misunderstanding the authority that You delegate to me. If it is Your will, allow me the opportunity to rectify circumstances in which my use of authority has impacted others to their detriment. Amen.

PRAYER PROMPT

"Rejoice in hope, be patient in tribulation, be constant in prayer." (Romans 12:12)

THEME: IDENTIFYING THE WILL OF GOD IN MY LIFE

LAW/GOSPEL

"And who knows whether you have not come to the kingdom for such a time as this?" (Esther 4:14)

OBJECTIVES FOR SESSION 4

I will recognize and accept God's Word as the final authority in my life.

I will understand that God prepares us for recognizing His will in my life.

WHAT WILL I LEARN?

I will learn that as a Christian, I am submissive to God when He rearranges my plans for His purposes.

HOW WILL I LEARN IT?

I will study about God nurturing Esther's spirit of obedience, preparing her to be submissive to His authority for the sake of others.

PREPARATION FOR STUDY: RELATIONAL UNDERSTANDING

I will recognize and accept God's Word as the final authority in my life.

The word *obedience* can cause a rush of conflicting emotions to flood our minds. The common understanding of the word *obedient* is "to be submissive to another person or to a system of rules." Obedience in various facets of our lives can be a struggle for us. As human beings, we want to do what we want, when and how we want; we want control. Obedience can make us feel weak and powerless or frustrated and stymied, causing us to feel the natural instinct of flight or fight. Taking flight would be to reject obedience, and fighting would be to wrestle for control.

In this lies the struggle of obedience, of putting ourselves in the control of another and allowing that person to guide our actions. The feeling of being defenseless and vulnerable is both uncomfortable and stressful. The world tells us we should strive for independence. We are taught from childhood, with good intention, that one day we will be on our own and will have to take care of ourselves. This can be a scary thought for a child, who at this tender stage is most comfortable believing that someone who loves him will take care of him, make all the hard decisions, defend and protect him, and assume responsibility for his physical and emotional needs. These earthly comforts are gifts given simply because we exist in the life of others who choose to love us. Most parents strive to be completely available for their children at any time, day or night, thereby fulfilling their God-given vocation as parents. As adult Christian children, we offer our help to our parents as they age. In some cases, we must provide not only the physical comfort of hugs and companionship but also a home, hands-on daily care, or financial support. Our care assures them that we appreciate their devotion to us.

As much as we need these earthly relationships, they are temporary; each person has an appointed time to depart this earth. Once our parents are gone, we might perceive ourselves as orphaned, no matter our age. When we were children, we were obedient to our parents, who loved us before we knew what love was or what it should look like or how it should feel. Our obedience to them was our first expression of love toward them.

As we mature in our understanding that God the Father chooses to love us and does so with a perfect love, we become willing to be obedient to Him. In our relationship with God, obedience includes mindfulness that all of the plans we make for ourselves are guided by His Law and will for us. In planning our days, weeks, and months, we must always consider that God may rearrange them. Just as we received care from our loved ones when we were little children, so our heavenly Father wants to provide all the love and care they did—and more. God is our ultimate provider of all good things. God never tells us that when we grow up, His days of caregiving will cease. In our relationship with Him, we never have to think about a time when He won't be in our lives to care for us, help us with hard decisions, or provide for us physically and spiritually. Take a moment and let this sink in. God was with us before we were born, He is with us throughout all our days on earth, He will be with us at the moment we depart this life, and He will be with us forever in our heavenly home. We will never be orphaned, because He loves us. Our response to His faithfulness is to be obedient to Him, just as a small child is to a beloved parent, because we are His children. He provides all that we need for life itself—our daily bread (Matthew 6:11).

I will understand that God prepares us for recognizing His will in my life.

God's time is outside of the realm of our existence. His timing in His dealings with us is always precise and always according to His will for us. Throughout our lives, God presents us with opportunities to submit to His will. This can be frightening, and often we respond by thinking, "I don't know if I am prepared for this." As students of God's Word, we remind one another that the will of God makes us ready to do what He asks of us.

Sometimes we may hesitate to do God's will in praying for another person, especially in the very moment when we recognize that God has put this person in our path. We may respond to a prayer request by saying, "I will pray for you." This is absolutely the right thing to say, but sometimes we can do more. We can pray for that person right there and then. He has presented this person to us for a reason, possibly beyond what we know at that moment. People need to hear us praying for them. It may feel awkward at first, but our words will be inspired by the Holy Spirit. God wants us to communicate with Him and to teach others how to talk to Him as well. We can teach others about the gift of prayer only if we model the behavior. What a gift we have to show others that our God is ever-present and ready to hear from us through prayers of faith for their needs, in their presence.

Esther was called to obey God's will in a way that threatened her very life. Her first response was the natural state of fear. With the help of her cousin Mordecai, who reminded her who she was as a believer in God's promise, she submitted to His will for her life. In session 3, we read that

God is the ultimate authority in our lives and that we are held accountable to Him for any authority He delegates to us. Once we have discovered that authority, we can recognize and accept how God wants us to use it for His purposes. God used many experiences to prepare Mordecai and Esther to be obedient to Him for a very specific purpose. God used these experiences to open their hearts and minds to recognize and accept the authority given to them. Through Mordecai and Esther's obedience to His Word, God fulfilled His promise of deliverance from the threat of destruction of their people. In this session, we will focus on Esther, but we start with Mordecai in order fully to understand that God wants us to know we can trust Him, no matter the circumstances. As we do, our willingness to be obedient to His guidance and instruction will increase.

PRAYER OF PREPARATION

Dear Lord, as I learn better to recognize and accept Your Word as the ultimate authority in my life, help me to understand that I can trust You to guide and carry me through all circumstances without worry or hesitation. Help me to hear the Holy Spirit as my helper and to feel secure and confident in Your love for me as my heavenly Father. Please help me to remember to trust in Your ways at all times, but especially when I feel weak and vulnerable. Through Your Word, guide me and keep me so I will develop a heart that is open and willing to be obedient to You and Your will for me. In Jesus' name, I pray. Amen.

OUR MENTOR—ESTHER

ABOUT THE TEXT

The story of Esther shows how God's plan was at work in positioning her to protect His people. Throughout this session, we will see how God rearranged the lives of both Esther and her cousin Mordecai in preparation for completing the work of salvation for them and the Israelites. Esther needed to recognize God's will and be obedient to His instruction. Her first thought was as an ordinary woman, looking at the natural limitations she would encounter. Later, she asked for support through prayer and sacrifice so that she could be guided by God. Esther offered her life as a sacrifice to help her people. This session explores how God prepares us to recognize that His will is to be the focus of our life at whatever the cost.

OUR MENTOR—ESTHER

Scripture Reading: the Book of Esther

1. How did God spiritually open a path for Esther to complete His will? See Esther 1.

   _____

   _____

   _____

   _____

   _____

   _____

2. What do I need to understand about God's plan for me? See Psalm 33:11; 139:16; Romans 8:28.

   _____

   _____

   _____

   _____

   _____

   _____

3. How did Mordecai demonstrate his submissiveness to God in acting as a parent in his cousin's Esther's life? See Esther 2:5–7.

   _____

   _____

   _____

   _____

   _____

4. When has God unexpectedly rearranged events, delegating authority to you to care for another on God's behalf? Examples include taking over a job at work, giving children a home, parenting someone else's child, or providing emotional support to another.

_____

_____

_____

_____

_____

_____

5. Why did Mordecai and Esther deceive the king by keeping her heritage a secret? See Esther 2:6–10.

_____

_____

_____

_____

_____

_____

6. Why did Mordecai conceal his Jewish heritage and command Esther to do the same? How did God redirect Mordecai in His will? See Esther 2:19–3:6.

_____

_____

_____

_____

_____

7. How did God use grief to answer their prayers for deliverance? See Esther 4:4–9; Psalm 34:17; Psalm 55:22.

_____

_____

_____

_____

_____

_____

8. How has God stopped an attack on you or others when you committed to His Word as the true authority in a situation that seemed threatening?

_____

_____

_____

_____

_____

_____

9. What did God awaken inside of Esther that led her to recognize and accept His will as her obligation to fulfill? See Esther 4:9–17; Isaiah 40:29.

_____

_____

_____

_____

_____

_____

SESSION CONCLUSION

At first glance, Esther appeared as though she was submissive to all authorities. We can follow a pattern that helps us understand her initial reaction to God's revelation to her. Esther was a dutiful follower. She lovingly complied with Mordecai's teaching as to what to believe and how to behave as a Jewish girl. Then she was under the charge of Hegai, the custodian of women in the king's palace, where she learned what to believe and how to behave as a member of the women's quarters in the palace. Finally, she became the wife to the king and was advised as how to behave as part of his province. At each stage of her development, Esther depended upon others for guidance on how to live and behave. This positioned her perfectly for recognizing and embracing God's revelation for what she needed to do. Esther's submissive heart, created by God, was fertile ground for her transformation from follower to leader at the opportune moment. Because Mordecai had trained her, Esther knew to ask her people to join her in fasting so she could focus clearly on God's will for her. Their participation in the fast was an act of faith and encouragement; they believed God would provide Esther with a clear resolution to the threat on their existence. God created in Esther a heart that was submissive to spiritual authority, which opened to His will at the time it was needed most. We live for Him, not ourselves, on this earth.

PRAYER STARTER

Dear Lord, help me to hold onto my confidence that You know me better than I know myself. I understand that I am asking You to give me experiences in my life that will strengthen my trust in Your wisdom. In Jesus' name and for His sake, I pray. Amen.

PRAYER PROMPT

"Likewise the Spirit helps us in our weakness, For we do not know what to pray for as we ought, but the Spirit Himself intercedes for us." (Romans 8:26)

THEME: # ACCOMPLISHING THE WILL OF GOD

LAW/GOSPEL

"He said to me, 'My grace is sufficient for you, for My power is made perfect in weakness.' Therefore I will boast all the more gladly of my weaknesses, so that the power of Christ may rest upon me." (2 Corinthians 12:9)

OBJECTIVE FOR SESSION 5

God will strengthen my faith during times of distress.

WHAT WILL I LEARN?

I will learn that when I am overwhelmed, I may call on God to strengthen me spiritually with both His grace and His help.

HOW WILL I LEARN IT?

I will explore the experiences of Paul and Silas, examining their intentional responses of separating themselves from the pressure of problems they encountered by choosing to stay focused on God's promises as He prepared them to accomplish His will for salvation in the world.

PREPARATION FOR STUDY: RELATIONAL UNDERSTANDING

God will strengthen my faith during times of distress.

Driven, ambitious, focused, and *determined* are just a few terms the world uses to describe the kind of person thought to have what it takes to stay the course when things get tough. Yet embracing these terms as the reason for success of any kind in any circumstance makes us question our personal abilities. In some cases, we start to believe that if these terms don't apply to us, then we don't have what it takes; we never had it and we never will. We may sense a false loss of power and control. We entertain the idea that something is wrong with us. We try to figure out ways to hurry our plans along; we might seek help from people who don't have our best interest in mind or who are confused. We sometimes pray to God in such a way that we are not seeking His will but wanting a confirmation of our own. When we pray in this way, we are telling God that He needs to come under our control. This behavior and attitude expresses what the world encourages and understands. The self-discipline understood by the world produces stress, frustration, and worry in an attempt to control events and circumstances that are beyond us. In contrast, in our relationship with God, self-discipline is a willingness to allow our behaviors, attitudes, feelings, thoughts, and language to come under the control of Christ, with the help of the Holy Spirit, to accomplish God's will. Jesus, the Son of God, was sent to earth for a specific purpose written by our heavenly Father. He modeled for us what accomplishing the will of God looks like. When we use the phrase "accomplishing God's will in my life," what are we really saying? We are saying that we want to be submissive to God's purposes. Submission requires intentional behavior of obedience to God. Furthermore, obedience requires a self-discipline that we cannot obtain of our own will.

The process of spiritual discipline throughout our lifetime makes us ready for eternal life. As students of the Word, we know that Jesus was challenged with everything a human could experience on earth, and yet He lived without sin. Christ made Himself a sacrifice so we would be saved by grace through the shedding of His blood. The truth of Christ's death on the cross is enough for the atonement of our sins. Attempting to live a life without sin is impossible for us due to the human nature we have been born into. Daily, we fall into sinful behaviors that challenge us, such as impulse control with speech and behavior, issues with dependability and accomplishing goals, sometimes refusing to listen, and even deliberate disobedience. However, being diligent in our efforts to allow God to use us for His purpose is within our control. As Christians, we must be willing to embrace intentional thinking about the situations that occur in our lives. Furthermore, we must reflect on His Word when choosing our behaviors and attitudes. Indeed, this intentional way of living our lives is not easy, but God wants us to honor Him by accepting His discipline, which is done out of love for us. Embracing the mindset that our God guides and directs each of us in every aspect of our lives so we are protected by His almighty arm is a wonderful gift. God gives us what we need to be disciplined in our behavior, language, and attitude and to stay diligent in our efforts—the Holy Spirit and the absolute truth of His promises in His Word.

In the study of Esther and Mordecai, we learned that any plan we make needs to align with God's ultimate plan for salvation. We saw how God used their vulnerability and obedience to show His power and grace, not only in their lives but also in the lives of all the Israelites and non-believers. The troubles experienced in the Book of Esther were not due to punishment; rather, God used human frailty for His purpose of showing His salvation.

This session centers on Paul and Silas and allows us to better understand how God strengthens us for His purposes using experiences in self-discipline.

PRAYER OF PREPARATION

Dear Lord, as I study about Your ways of preparing me to serve Your purposes, help me to remember that although I have free will, ultimately Your will for me is eternal life with You in heaven. With the help of the Holy Spirit, help me to remember that my relationship with You requires that I be willing to be submissive to Your teachings for my own sake. Please help me to accept Your discipline as an expression of Your love and care for me. Help me to remember that my problems and concerns can establish a new path for me to grow closer to You. In Jesus' name, I pray. Amen.

OUR MENTOR—PAUL

ABOUT THE TEXT

The apostle Paul, once known for zealous attempts to stop the spread of the Gospel, became an instrument of God for the salvation of souls. God sought Paul and shaped his attitude, behavior, language, and work, conforming him to His plan for Paul's life and ministry and for the salvation of all nations (Acts 9:19–22). God called Paul to go to the region of Macedonia, where Paul and Silas found themselves in circumstances that could have caused them to fail in their ministry. They sensed extreme emotional and mental pressures as soon as they arrived, starting with the relentless ranting of a demon-possessed girl. In this session, we learn the intentional behavior and attitude needed during times of overwhelming pressure to help us stay focused on God instead of on circumstances.

OUR MENTOR—PAUL

Scripture Reading: Acts 16

1. What events confirm for us that God prepared the way for Paul, Silas, and Timothy upon their arrival to the region of Macedonia? See Acts 16:1–15.

    _____

    _____

    _____

    _____

    _____

    _____

2. When has God redirected me, or put me in the right place at the right time, and provided me with confirmation that I was where He wanted me to be?

    _____

    _____

    _____

    _____

    _____

    _____

3. What was the cause of Paul's distress in the marketplace with Silas? See Acts 16:16–24.

    _____

    _____

    _____

    _____

    _____

    _____

4. What was the reaction from the owners of the slave girl and others in the marketplace once the demon left her? See Acts 16:19–24.

    _____

    _____

    _____

    _____

    _____

5. How did the response of Paul and Silas to being put in prison show their belief that God is real? See Acts 16:25–40.

    _____

    _____

    _____

    _____

    _____

6. What do the prison and chains that bound Paul and Silas symbolize for me?

    _____

    _____

    _____

    _____

    _____

7. How did God's deliverance of Paul and Silas affect the jailer?

    _____

    _____

    _____

    _____

    _____

SESSION CONCLUSION

God rearranged the plans of Paul and Silas and placed them in another region to serve for His purposes. This change was rich with trouble and with miracles, but God had prepared them for this work. All the work done in Macedonia was for the salvation of many people, to the glory of God. Paul and Silas prayed to God, letting Him know that they had not forgotten His promises to them. We can do the same in any situation. God wants us to remember His love for us, His promises to us, and His authority over any threat, challenge, or situation. Paul and Silas held on to our mighty Father in heaven as their deliverer. All of these events had to occur just as they did, with God using Paul as His instrument of choice (Acts 9:15–16). What was the will of God that Paul and Silas were to accomplish in this story? The answer is divine rescue and salvation!

PRAYER STARTER

Dear Lord, there are times when I am burdened by circumstances that cause me to fear and feel helpless. With the comfort of Your promises to help me, I strive to keep my faith in You with the help of the Holy Spirit, so I can escape the pressure I feel. Help me to see clearly the path You have ordered for my deliverance. I pray in Jesus' name. Amen.

PRAYER PROMPT

"Be pleased, O LORD, to deliver me! O LORD, make haste to help me!" (Psalm 40:13)

THEME: SEEKING AN INTIMATE RELATIONSHIP WITH GOD

LAW/GOSPEL

"You knitted me together in my mother's womb. . . . Wonderful are Your works; my soul knows it very well. My frame was not hidden from You." (Psalm 139:13–15)

OBJECTIVE FOR SESSION 6

I will understand that only God offers real intimacy.

WHAT WILL I LEARN?

I will learn what is needed to have an intimate relationship with God, mediated by the study of His Holy Word and by partaking in the Sacrament, as He communicates His plans to me so that my life is aligned with His will.

HOW WILL I LEARN IT?

I will explore the characteristics of the relationship God had with David in order to learn that spiritual intimacy requires me to spend time in study, prayer, and worship, and to receive Him in the Lord's Supper.

PREPARATION FOR STUDY: RELATIONAL UNDERSTANDING

I will understand that only God offers real intimacy.

According to common understanding in the world, the word *intimacy* is associated with marriage or friendship. In these relationships, we have certain expectations, such as feeling a sense of permanence, feeling emotionally safe and secure, believing this person will always be on our side and will defend us against others who might attack our character or physical being, and being able to trust this person, to name just a few. We make lofty plans with the other person, believing that our relationship will last indefinitely. We find real comfort in believing we have found a person with whom we can bond for life. God provided Adam with Eve for the very purpose of assuring that he would not be lonely. However, when we place all of our trust in mere mortals, expecting them to manage their own lives in concert with attending to our weaknesses, needs, and desires, then disappointment is inevitable. In some cases, we argue that we should not have to tell them what we want or need because they should already know. We may never realize that what we are really doing is demanding godlike characteristics from a fellow human being. Now that is something to think seriously about—expecting godlike characteristics from a fellow sinner!

A song of David, Psalm 62, tells us that only God can bring salvation to us. David describes God as "my rock and my salvation, my fortress" (v. 1) and proclaims that his salvation and refuge rests on the shoulders of God. Furthermore, we are told to "trust in Him at all times, . . . pour out your heart before Him" (v. 8) This means we express to God our secrets, fears, dreams, and passions. David reminds us that the things of the world are uncertain and will waste away. In other words, the intimacy we so desperately want to experience cannot be found in this temporary world, but only in the permanent relationship we have with God. With the help of the Holy Spirit that Jesus sent to us, we have access to a permanent, lifelong relationship of intimacy with our Creator. In our relationship with Him, we can be honest about our feelings and about who we are. We can trust Him completely with all of our concerns. God wants to redirect our energy and understanding so that we know that He is our source for everything. Of course, we still have close relationships with other people, but we understand that only God can attend to all our needs. God is always available to us through the genuine, loving relationship He established with us in our Baptism. This relationship requires intentional behaviors to maintain it. This is no different than what we expect from one another.

God created relationships for His purpose of connecting to us and for us to connect to Him. In Romans 1:18–22, we read that those who don't know the Gospel can still know, through the creation, that God exists and thus have no excuse not to be in a relationship with Him. His divine nature is shown to all of us throughout creation; therefore, there is no excuse for choosing to dishonor Him or neglecting to give thanks to Him. We must be willing to open our heart and trust Him to hear our confessions privately in prayer and corporately in worship. After we confess our transgressions with a sincere heart of repentance, we receive His gift of forgiveness and we change our behavior toward Him by making time for Him in our lives through prayer, worship, and study of His Word. We behave in the same way in a human relationship that is of value to us. Our loved ones and caregivers share with and provide for us. We would not dishonor them by neglecting the benefits we have received from their relationship with us or by neglecting to express thankfulness for their presence in our lives. In comparison, we have all felt the pain of rejection at times when we have attempted to show our love, friendship, and devotion to someone who chooses to ignore our presence yet continues to receive the goodness of our efforts. Yet even after all our neglectful behaviors, after we have ignored or dishonored Him, God listens when we pray to Him in Jesus' name (see 1 John 5:15). Relationship restored, we again listen to Him by studying His Word and by hearing the Gospel of Jesus Christ preached in the Divine Service.

We understand that a relationship with another person requires certain attributes to remain stable and secure. Those same attributes are present in our relationship with God. When relationships falter, it is due to lack of attention, callous attitude, lack of cooperation, and lack of respect on the part of one or both parties. Our relationship with God is no different. As we study the relationship David had with God, we notice that David put up no barriers, such as pride, rebellion, or inattentiveness, that would distance him from the full blessings, instruction, and protection of God. David was honest and humble before the Lord. Perceiving David as our mentor for how to be in a personal spiritual relationship with God provides us with the gift of feeling stable, secure, loved, and safe within the knowledge that our Creator cares for us and provides us with what we truly need in this life.

PRAYER OF PREPARATION

Dear Lord, I want the same kind of comfort that David experienced in his relationship with You. Help me to be mindful of ways my attitude and behavior can develop barriers between us. Please keep me attentive to my relationship to You, and help me to maintain constant communication in prayer and in worship to allow me to be guided by You. With the help of the Holy Spirit, I pray that You never allow me to stray from Your loving arms. In Jesus' name, I pray. Amen.

OUR MENTOR—DAVID

ABOUT THE TEXT

God sent Samuel to anoint a replacement king for Israel. The prophet sought another king based on his human traits, but when David appeared before Samuel, the Lord said, "Anoint him, for this is he" (1 Samuel 16:12). Three events in David's life allow us to examine the differences between how he was perceived as a son of Jesse and who he truly was as a man of God: his anointing, his ability to reassure Saul, and his defeat of Goliath. We learn in this session that God knows us differently than we can ever know one another. God tells us this in His message to Samuel. "Do not look on his appearance. . . . For the LORD sees not as man sees: man looks on the outward appearance, but the LORD looks on the heart" (1 Samuel 16:7).

OUR MENTOR—DAVID

Scripture Reading: 1 Samuel 16:1–17:37

1. Why did God send Samuel to the tent of Jesse? See 1 Samuel 16:1–13.

   _____

   _____

   _____

   _____

   _____

2. What did God explain to Samuel about his assumption for choosing David's brother Eliab?

   _____

   _____

   _____

   _____

   _____

3. What caused God to say, "Anoint him, for this is he" (1 Samuel 16:12), in reference to David?

   _____

   _____

   _____

   _____

   _____

4. What was the importance of David's response to Eliab and Saul about fighting Goliath? See 1 Samuel 17:20–37.

   _____

   _____

   _____

   _____

5. When a person has an intimate relationship with God, certain characteristics are present. What are they? See Psalm 62:1–2; 63:1; 1 John 1:5–10; James 1:1–8; 1 Peter 3:12; Proverbs 3:5–6.

_____

_____

_____

_____

_____

6. What human limitations become evident when we examine David's capability in his early life from a human perspective? See 1 Samuel 16:11; 17:1–37.

_____

_____

_____

_____

_____

7. When have I prayed to God for His direction regarding selecting someone or being selected for service in church, work, or community?

_____

_____

_____

_____

_____

SESSION CONCLUSION

Our relationship with God is personal, and our response to Him includes trust, love, and honesty. We cannot have a genuine relationship with another person without each person recognizing that these attributes are critical. Therefore, it is impossible to be in a genuine relationship to God unless we are truthful with Him, tell Him all things good or bad, hear Him speak through His Word, and trust His guidance revealed in that Word. In this world, we are like David, living a life filled with Goliath-size challenges. God is merciful to David because He looks inward on his heart. The heart is a mystery to us because we cannot know what is in it; however, the heart is not hidden from God. God knew that David would not turn to false gods but would stay true to Him, no matter the cost. David's time in the mountains tending and defending his father's sheep strengthened his faith in God's ability to deliver him from any challenge. Others may have perceived David's time alone in the mountains as unfruitful, even wasteful, resulting in their perception that he was without ability or value, but he was exactly where God wanted him. David was not alone, and God proved it to him during each and every life challenge. God had been increasing David's faith in His ability to provide everything he needed to recognize and fulfill His divine will when called upon. David was not perfect (just as we are not perfect) and when he failed he repented, but he finished God's plan. David always prayed for guidance and instruction from God and waited to hear from Him with unwavering faith that he would receive an answer. He never quit, doubted, hesitated, or argued with God as each required behavior was revealed to him. At times, he was afraid, just as we are, but he did not allow himself to focus on his fear.

The apostle Paul reminded the Jewish people in Antioch of David's relationship with God, saying "He raised up David to be their king, of whom he testified and said, 'I have found in David the son of Jesse a man after My heart, who will do all My will.' Of this man's offspring God has brought to Israel a Savior, Jesus, as He promised" (Acts 13:22–23).

PRAYER STARTER

Dear Lord, I am not perfect, but I want to have a more intimate relationship with You. With the help of the Holy Spirit, open my heart through the study of Your Word, and continue to bring me closer to You. Assure me of Your faithfulness to me in every challenge I may face. And strengthen my faith in the resurrection of Your Son, our Lord and Savior, in whose name I pray. Amen.

PRAYER PROMPT

"But as for you, continue in what you have learned and have firmly believed, knowing from whom you learned it and how from childhood you have been acquainted with the sacred writings, which are able to make you wise for salvation through faith in Christ Jesus." (2 Timothy 3:14–15)

THEME: **FOLLOWING GOD'S REVELATIONS ONE BY ONE**

LAW/GOSPEL

"Many are the plans in the mind of a man, but it is the purpose of the LORD that will stand." (Proverbs 19:21)

OBJECTIVE FOR SESSION 7

I will understand how God reveals His plan for living in the world.

WHAT WILL I LEARN?

I will learn that leaning on my human understanding can interfere with my belief to receive the gifts God has for me.

HOW WILL I LEARN IT?

I will study the beginnings of Abraham's relationship with God and the experiences that taught Abraham to trust fully in God's instruction and guidance, regardless of his human understanding.

PREPARATION FOR STUDY: RELATIONAL UNDERSTANDING

I will understand how God reveals His plan for living in the world.

The idea of hijacking may strike fear in us as we prepare to travel. We may think about airplanes being taken over by terrorists, gang affiliates, or others who resort to this desperate action. We comfort ourselves by telling ourselves these situations are few and far between, making the experience seem remote. We would never think of ourselves as hijackers. After all, a hijacker, according to common understanding, is a person who takes over an activity and uses it for a different purpose. It's something that "bad" people do to others; when caught, they are judged, punished, jailed, and shamed because they dared to interfere with or disrupt the order of things. They offended the authorities and caused distress to those affected by their actions, making them feel vulnerable. But let's think about this word *hijacker* as it relates to God and His plans for His purposes.

God created this world, and He created order so that certain experiences (such as the sun and moon rising and setting, weather patterns, and seasons) can be expected. He also created us for the purpose of having a relationship with Him, our loving Father in heaven. Just as we do for our children, God has plans for us to keep us safe, and yet He also gives us free will to make plans for the life He gives us. We must exercise caution and refrain from the urge to hijack His plan for us and follow our own will. We can have the ability to steer clear of this urge only by knowing Him through hearing His Word proclaimed and by studying His Word in the Bible. We grow in our understanding of His plans for us by meditating on His promises to provide for us, protect us from the devil, and always be with us, regardless of what we experience or see. When we faithfully submit to His will, our thoughts are changed and we are able to stay the course He has set before us.

The urge to hijack God's plan is rooted in sin. The anxiousness, impatience, fear, frustration, or anxiety we feel during times of difficulty and uncertainty come from lack of trust in our heavenly Father. We say things such as, "I just needed to do something; I got so nervous; I got tired of waiting." Not only does the urge to hijack God's plan produce distance between us and Him, but it also produces emotional, spiritual, and physical havoc in our lives and relationships with others. Hijacking His plan is an act of disobedience, because through this behavior we are saying that our plan is better; we are placing ourselves above God.

Abraham felt this urge to hijack the plan God had for him because of what he was feeling and seeing. In this session, we will explore how Abraham learned to trust God's plan for his life regardless of the circumstances; through this session, we will learn to understand ourselves better. It will help us to stay the course until the next step in God's plan is revealed. Becoming more aware of our urge to hijack His plan for us will help us resist it and help redirect our steps to align with His.

PRAYER OF PREPARATION

Dear Lord, You know where I am in my spiritual growth and maturity. Help me to remember that my part in Your plan is revealed gradually throughout my life. As Your child, I need not try to figure out Your hidden or full plans for me. Instead, I submit to Your instruction moment by moment, as it is revealed to me day by day. With the help of the Holy Spirit, I will recognize Your undeserved favor and will receive Your teaching through Your Word and by Your answers to my prayers. Help me to accept Your answers, even if they bring suffering, disappointment, and sacrifice. Please help me to remember that through these instructional moments in my life, You are preparing me to understand how to honor You with my life. In Jesus' name, I pray. Amen.

OUR MENTOR—ABRAHAM

ABOUT THE TEXT

God extends His blessing of salvation to Abraham, a man with pagan beliefs, offering him eternal salvation. Out of His mercy and grace, God revealed to Abraham His plan for his life. Abraham gave up his self-reliance and saw the Promised Land at last, as he learned to trust the Lord. During his struggle to mature in his faith, Abraham experienced setbacks and trials that allowed him to develop an unwavering trusting relationship in God. This session illustrates the limitations associated with leaning on human understanding instead of God's wisdom.

OUR MENTOR—ABRAHAM

Scripture Reading: Genesis 12:1–13:4

1. What was the promise God made to Abraham (Abram) that clearly helps us understand His mercy and grace, extended to rescue him from his sins? See Genesis 12:1–3.

   _____

   _____

   _____

   _____

   _____

   _____

2. Why did Abraham believe what he heard? See Acts 16:14; Luke 11:28.

   _____

   _____

   _____

   _____

   _____

3. What specific actions did Abraham take as a result of hearing the Word of God? See Genesis 12:4–7.

   _____

   _____

   _____

   _____

   _____

4. When have I rejected opportunities because I experienced immediate discomfort or uneasiness and then realized they were against God's will for my life?

_____

_____

_____

_____

_____

_____

5. What was God doing in Abraham as a result of difficult experiences that caused him to return to God's will? See Matthew 6:25–34.

_____

_____

_____

_____

_____

_____

6. What do I need to remember during times of stress? See James 1:2–4; Proverbs 3:5–6; Philippians 4:6–7; Psalm 56:3.

_____

_____

_____

_____

_____

7. What did Abraham do once God rescued him from the Egyptian pharaoh? See Genesis 13:1–4.

    _____

    _____

    _____

    _____

    _____

    _____

8. What must I truly believe about God's plan for me? See Romans 8:28; Colossians 1:16.

    _____

    _____

    _____

    _____

    _____

    _____

SESSION CONCLUSION

God identified Abraham as the father of the nations of the earth. God prepared Abraham's heart to recognize Him and willingly embrace His Word. Abraham's process of maturing as a believer is no different from ours. There will be mishaps, misunderstandings, rebellions, and impulse-control issues that will cause us trouble, because our natural behavior is contrary to God's will for us. Some specific behaviors may appear to work for us in the natural world but may have no use or value when we know God as our heavenly Father and provider. Abraham was a wealthy man (Genesis 12:16; 13:1–2; 13:6) and was accustomed to being the decision-maker regarding the well-being of his family and larger household. Abraham did exactly what we have done and will continue to do at various stages of our faith journey—mess up. But God, who is faithful, continues to forgive, rescue, and love His children. God has mercy on all of us, and He extends His love as a means to rescue us from our sin. His ultimate plan has always been to rescue us from the eternal damnation sin causes. His plan is unconditional. Just as God fulfilled His promise to deliver Abraham, despite his sin, so He keeps His promise to deliver us. "God shows His love for us in that while we were still sinners, Christ died for us" (Romans 5:8).

PRAYER STARTER

Dear Lord Jesus, thank You for Your patience as I mature in faith, expanding my understanding of who You are and how I am to have a relationship with You. Thank You for rescuing me and returning me to You when I need You most. Amen.

PRAYER PROMPT

"Blessed is the man who trusts in the LORD, whose trust is the LORD." (Jeremiah 17:7)

THEME: ALLOWING GOD TO RECTIFY MY SELF-PERCEPTION

LAW/GOSPEL

"If we say we have not sinned, we make Him a liar, and His word is not in us." (1 John 1:10)

OBJECTIVE FOR SESSION 8

I will understand that we love God for who He is, not because of blessings gained or to avoid punishment.

WHAT WILL I LEARN?

I will learn that God empowers me to live in faith, even when I don't fully understand His ways.

HOW WILL I LEARN IT?

I will examine conversations that Job had with God as God revealed to him that what He does is not affected by any human effort.

PREPARATION FOR STUDY: RELATIONAL UNDERSTANDING

I will understand that we love God for who He is, not because of blessings gained or to avoid punishment.

We have all been guilty of wondering why something has happened, is happening, or did not happen. In pain, agony, fear, or despair, we ask, "What did I do? What did someone else do?" At other times, we cry out, "God, why did You let this happen? What caused this illness, disappointment, or death?" We become defiant because we believe there has to be a reason. This attitude may result in our becoming confrontational toward people in positions of authority, such as parents, teachers, doctors, or governing officials. We expect them to control situations that are fearsome to us. "How can they not have an answer that helps us understand?" This attitude can easily spill over into our relationship with God. We may find ourselves flipping through the Bible, searching for answers. We get annual medical exams, take our vitamins, exercise regularly, drinks lots of water, and get rest; but our bodies still fall ill. Out of compassion for others, we may get caught in the frenzy of trying to provide an answer for them. The only real answer we can provide is "I don't know." (Their response may be, "Well, you're a Christian; what does it say in the Bible?") In other situations, we might say, "It's God's will." (Then their response may be, "What do you mean it's God's will? How can this be God's will?") If we ourselves are struggling with a bad situation, others may ask, "Why would God allow bad things to happen to good Christian people? You have been going to church all your life; why you?" Yes, we are Christians, and with our faith comes our understanding that life this side of heaven is imperfect and broken but we are accountable to stay diligent to behaviors that we know keep us close to God.

The apostle Paul tells us in Romans 12:1 that we are to present our bodies as a living sacrifice to God. Our suffering and pain may come as a means for our personal good, or it may be for the sake of others, so that they may be strengthened and encouraged during their own time of struggle. For instance, when we need surgery or other medical treatment, God may be positioning us to show our faith in His ability to bring us through this trial for the sake of our relatives, friends, medical team, or fellow church members who may be mentally wrestling with a similar issue. At other times, God may choose to bring us home to Him. In both instances, we must choose to believe that His authoritative decision is best for each of us. We are accustomed to ask questions when things happen in this world, guided by the example of the news media that dig into the details and causes of disasters and violent situations. In school, we learn to employ *who*, *what*, *where*, *when*, *why*, and *how* questions in an effort to find answers. We promise one another that we will not be satisfied until we know the answers, the *why* of our circumstances.

Job is a man no different than any one of us. He is trying to live a life that is acceptable in God's eyes. But just like us, Job misunderstands who God is and the type of relationship He wants to have with us. Studying the various human emotions expressed by Job during the most difficult times in his life, we learn that he never wavered in seeking God. As challenges in our personal lives create waves of emotions that send us searching for answers, we, too, can be anchored in our belief that God loves us.

PRAYER OF PREPARATION

Dear Lord, thank You for the opportunity to become more familiar with the story of Job. Through Your ministry to him, I am convinced that even during times of illness, struggles, and chaos, You are with me. Help me to remember that any challenges I face can be dealt with as long as I have faith in You as my Redeemer and rely on Your plan for my life. As I struggle with my emotions, never let the Holy Spirit leave me; minister to me and anchor me to Your everlasting love. In Jesus' name, I pray. Amen.

OUR MENTOR—JOB

ABOUT THE TEXT

Job was wealthy and healthy, and he loved his family. Job is described as blameless and righteous; however, he misunderstood his relationship with God. Satan accused Job of loving God and serving Him in an attempt to receive God's reward for obedience and avoid punishment for disobedience. To prove the opposite, God gave Satan permission to test Job's faith. We will focus our session on Job's interactions with God after great loss and as he was suffering from an illness that kept him bedridden. This session will describe misunderstandings about humankind's relationship with God; through this session, we will learn that there is no requirement for us to earn God's favor. Our heavenly Father loves us and wants us to know Him through study of His Holy Word. As we better understand the character of God, we learn to trust that His favor is given to each of us according to His will.

OUR MENTOR—JOB

Scripture Reading: Job 1–2; 42

1. Where in the Bible do we see God grant favor at His discretion? See Jonah 3:6–4:11; Genesis 4:3–7; Luke 1:28–38.

    _____

    _____

    _____

    _____

    _____

    _____

2. Where in the Bible do we see God grant favor in response to faithfulness? See Daniel 1:8–17; Hebrew 11:5; Acts 7:44–46; Acts 2:42–47; Luke 2:46–52.

    _____

    _____

    _____

    _____

    _____

3. What caused Job to make excessive offerings to God after the feasts of his family? See Job 1:1–12.

    _____

    _____

    _____

    _____

    _____

4. What was Job's reaction toward God after Satan took his property and children? See Job 1:13–22.

_____

_____

_____

_____

_____

_____

5. During Job's illness, what was the additional attack challenging his faith? See Job 2:1–10.

_____

_____

_____

_____

_____

_____

6. What was the reaction of Job's three friends when they arrived to visit him? See Job 2:11–13.

_____

_____

_____

_____

_____

_____

Note to Reader: A large portion of the Book of Job depicts Job's three friends as they attempted to comprehend his circumstances, with each showing how his own human reasoning was limited. Job submitted to his own lack of understanding, in concert with realizing that God is in control.

7. Where in the Bible does God grant favor in response to righteousness in suffering and self-sacrifice? See 1 Peter 3:17; Job 42:1–6.

_____

_____

_____

_____

_____

_____

8. What did God do for Job as an act of grace, not as a reward for faithfulness? See Job 42:10–17.

_____

_____

_____

_____

_____

_____

9. When have I expressed disappointment or anger toward God because I experienced hard times financially, such as paying credit card or utility bills, paying off student debt, medical bills, mortgage payments, car repairs, or other unexpected expenses?

_____

_____

_____

_____

_____

SESSION CONCLUSION

After studying Job's story, you may begin to think of your experiences as God's story of love, mercy, character building, and grace, instead of perceiving your problems as your own story. Remembering the trials that God has brought us through is a personal blessing that is meant to be shared. Others need to hear that God can help them too. We should not view our difficult experiences as times we don't want to recall or talk about or as things about which we are embarrassed. Rather, these experiences can move us to give God the glory He deserves. Think of it this way: if we don't want to talk about the goodness of the Lord in our difficult times, then we are keeping His mercy for us and our love for Him a secret. Jesus wants us to spread the Good News of the Gospel, not keep it a secret. "For whoever is ashamed of Me and of My words, of him will the Son of Man be ashamed when He comes in His glory and the glory of the Father and of the holy angels" (Luke 9:26). God communed with Job through the work of the Holy Spirit as He responded to his cries and self-pity. God spoke to Job as he had hoped (Job 23:6–7) and as Job's friend Elihu had assured (Job 33:14–17). God did not abandon Job, even though Job believed he was alone because of his sin. Although Job had been ranting (Job 16:3), God confronted Job with His love while flooding Job's mind with both challenges and unthought-of questions, forcing him to ponder the greatness of our heavenly Father (Job 38:1–40:2; 40:6–24). God's questions bring to mind His creative power and everlasting presence in all of the uncertainties of our lives. God's lesson calls us all to respect that His blueprint for all creation is not dependent on our cooperation. In His response, we see how God granted favor to Job by restraining judgment on him and extending His divine grace. Afterward, Job confessed and repented (Job 42:1–6), and he prayed for his three friends to be forgiven (Job 42:7–9). Job's friends had misunderstood how God was working through him to bring a testimony of His goodness and grace to others.

We cannot live as human beings without participating in sin. It is impossible. Why? In Romans 5:12, the apostle Paul explains that sin came into the world through the sinful act of Adam, the first mortal man. His mortal sin spread to all of humankind. In other words, we have inherited mortality from our parents, who inherited it from the world's first parents,

Adam and Eve. Along with Adam's mortality, we have inherited his guilt and desire to sin. To perceive ourselves as without sin is itself a sinful act of disobedience.

We can witness God's favor in our lives as approval, acceptance, affection, and blessings in response to prayer, at His pleasure or discretion; however, we can also witness His favor in the midst of suffering and sacrifices. Our faith tells us to cling to the truth of our heavenly Father and to continue to believe that He is present with us as we face issues, tests, and trials that may threaten our very lives. Even during common experiences, God is working in our individual lives for our good according to His purposes. We can acknowledge His favor by acknowledging "our daily bread," that is, food and shelter, and by remembering our Baptism. Although we cannot earn favor from God—it is under His sovereign authority to be given—we can still identify times in our lives that show us that God's favor is real.

PRAYER STARTER

Dear Lord, I submit to Your divine authority over my life as I seek Your love, grace, and mercy, through Your Son, Christ Jesus. Help me to remember that all of my experiences as Your child are for Your glory and for my good. With the help of the Holy Spirit, help me to understand that I am a living sacrifice to be used for Your purpose. In Jesus' name, I pray. Amen.

PRAYER PROMPT

"Remember not the sins of my youth or my transgressions; according to Your steadfast love remember me, for the sake of Your goodness, O Lord!" (Psalm 25:7)

THEME: STAYING COMMITTED TO LIVING OUT GOD'S WILL

LAW/GOSPEL

"O favored one, the Lord is with you!" (Luke 1:28)

OBJECTIVE FOR SESSION 9

I will learn that God strengthens us to survive a lifetime of difficulties by His divine grace.

I will understand that faith allows us to recognize God's favor and mercy in every aspect of our lives.

WHAT WILL I LEARN?

I will learn that God's grace is sufficient for me to live according to His Word.

HOW WILL I LEARN IT?

I will study how God nurtured a relationship with Mary, the mother of Jesus, as He strengthened her commitment to trust in His Word, according to His purpose for her life and for the salvation of humankind.

PREPARATION FOR STUDY: RELATIONAL UNDERSTANDING

I will learn that God strengthens us to survive a lifetime of difficulties by His divine grace.

The world seeks to praise us for looking after ourselves in all circumstances. The world wants to know how we overcame obstacles. Media personalities ask, "Who is the hero?" As human beings, created with natural compassion, it is our desire to be of service to one another in times of need. It is good to want to help others in any way we can, but we must remember that it is never our personal ability that accomplishes these things. As believers, we are ever mindful of God's presence in all situations and circumstances; it is He who determines our abilities. The question we must ask is this: what is the world really looking for when it wants to identify a hero in a difficult situation? It is asking people to take credit for God's work of salvation. The world wants us to believe that God is no longer in authority, no longer in the business of keeping His promise to be with us throughout our lives. Instead, we are encouraged to believe that we have to find ways to save and protect ourselves from the uncertainties of this world. As believers, we resist embracing this way of thinking and see it for what it is—Satan's attempt to separate us from God by making us doubt His sovereignty.

With every opportunity, we point others to God's Word and promise of salvation. "In His hand is the life of every living thing and the breath of all mankind" (Job 12:10). There is no other reason for our very existence than His divine plan for us to have a relationship with Him as our Creator and heavenly Father. "For His invisible attributes, namely, His eternal power and divine nature, have been clearly perceived, ever since the creation of the world, in the things that have been made. So they are without excuse" (Romans 1:20). God provides all that we need to live on this earth. We experience grace from God because He wants to take care of us. "The LORD is good to all, and His mercy is over all that He has made" (Psalm 145:9).

Believers and nonbelievers alike receive the goodness of His blessings. The sun warms our days; moonlight softens the intense darkness of the night; rainwater provides all the nutrients needed by our bodies to function, and He replenishes it at His will; He provides food for us in the form of plants and animals. Nature and all its creation is designed by God for Him to reveal Himself to all people. We all receive these natural provisions from our heavenly Father simply because He loves us. Sadly, we all are guilty of taking these gifts for granted. Still, God offers us His undeserved mercy and grace. "For I delivered to you as of first importance what I also received: that Christ died for our sins in accordance with the Scriptures"

(1 Corinthians 15:3). Paul is telling us that our first order of business in this world is to understand that God came to us in the form of Jesus Christ, who fulfilled the Law in our place by dying on the cross for the sin of the world. This act is God's ultimate provision for us.

We respond to this gift by sharing God's story of salvation. We tell our personal experience with Christ as our Savior. "For I am not ashamed of the gospel, for it is the power of God for salvation to everyone who believes, to the Jew first and also to the Greek" (Romans 1:16). Sharing our personal testimony of God's love and care for us during trials and tribulations is the purest way to introduce others to His gift of salvation from sin, which provides us with everlasting life with Him in heaven. "If you confess with your mouth that Jesus is Lord and believe in your heart that God raised Him from the dead, you will be saved. For with the heart one believes" (Romans 10:9–10).

We can do this only by trusting God's Word and reflecting on what He does for us during painful, confusing, and dark times. And the only way to trust His Word is to study it. Spending time in God's Word allows us to know Him as our heavenly Father and Jesus as our Savior. Through studying, we learn that our relationship with Jesus is offered to us out of love. We learn to trust Him, praise Him, follow Him, and pray to Him. Jesus is our hero! He is our salvation. He is our rescuer and friend. Jesus presented Himself as a divine sacrifice for us.

"And I will ask the Father, and He will give you another Helper, to be with you forever" (John 14:16). Jesus went before our Father to send the Holy Spirit to us as our Comforter and Helper until He returns to us. With the help of the Holy Spirit, we are strengthened in our faith in Jesus' power to do the impossible for us. Only the Holy Spirit can provide true peace in the middle of chaos and protection in the middle of a storm. Only the Helper can give guidance and instruction to lead us out of confusion.

I will understand that faith allows us to recognize God's favor and mercy in every aspect of our lives.

It is extremely difficult to see our children in mental, emotional, or physical pain. Sometimes we may respond to their pain with panic. All of a sudden, we want to run. Or we feel as if we are about to be run down, as if we are standing in front of an oncoming car or train. At other times, it feels as if we are standing at the opening of a tunnel, and the darkness inside absorbs the light and snuffs it out. Who can help us? We hear ourselves making statements such as, "I don't know how we are going to get through this." The answer is "only with the help of God." God is the source of our strength, comfort, protection, and reassurance. He shows the world His everlasting salvation through our situations.

"Even to your old age I am He, and to gray hairs I will carry you. I have made, and I will bear; I will carry and will save" (Isaiah 46:4). God is rescuing, saving, sustaining, protecting, and resolving circumstances in our lives every minute of every day. "We know that for those who love God all things work together for good, for those who are called according to His purpose" (Romans 8:28).

God's help comes in many forms: pastoral care, counseling, therapy, and medical assistance. He is always thinking about us, always making provisions for us, and He will never abandon us. When we repeat Psalm 23, we are thanking God for being who He is: our Shepherd, who is teaching, comforting, providing for, and protecting us. We are praising Him for His guidance to keep us out of emotional, mental, and physical danger. "The valley of the shadow of death" (Psalm 23:4) describes all those frightening situations, including panic attacks. Panic attacks can create even more turmoil than physical danger, because they happen inside of us.

Many of our biblical mentors experienced situations that probably caused them to feel a sense of urgency. Their intent to know God through the Scriptures helped them to focus on Him. Hearing His Word helped them recognize His provisions, which were unique to their circumstances, and they remained committed to trust in His covenant promises. We seek the Lord's strength during our times of weakness. We don't need to wonder where our strength to cope with difficulties will come from. Our faith, a gift of the Holy Spirit, makes us ready and able to live out all of our experiences because the Lord is always with us "to the end of the age" (Matthew 28:20). And Psalm 139:7–10 assures us that God is present in every situation and everywhere!

Mary, the mother of Jesus, experienced a life filled with difficulties as she shared the pain of her Son, Jesus Christ, as the world rejected Him. Yet in her suffering, she reflected the glory of Christ in His mission to bring His saving works to the hopeless. In Colossians 1:24–29, Paul tells us that all people suffer because of sin in the world. However, the suffering endured by Christians is uniquely characterized as being for the sake of Christ. In Mary's life, we see the relationship between her commitment to live according to God's Word (Luke 1:38) and the fulfillment of God's promise sent in the flesh to humankind for divine salvation (Isaiah 9:6–7). This special encounter shows us that she was the first of all humankind to know that the Old Testament prophecy (Genesis 3:15) was about to be fulfilled for our salvation. The Lord God nurtured and strengthened Mary's faith long before she heard the message of Gabriel. It was her faith in God's Word that kept her in prayer to our heavenly Father. He provided favor that strengthened her commitment to trust in His Holy Word according to her experience.

PRAYER OF PREPARATION

Dear Lord, I know there will be both joy and sorrow in my life on earth. Help me to be humble in my heart to accept that I cannot manage on my own. I ask You to strengthen me, with the help of the Holy Spirit, to maintain my personal commitment to living out Your will in my life according to Your Word. Keep me disciplined in thought, word, and deed always to express that it is You looking after me in all situations. Help me, Lord, during situations that cause me to panic, that I may run into Your loving arms in prayer. Thank You, Lord, for not leaving me to look after myself. In Jesus' name, I pray. Amen.

OUR MENTOR—MARY

ABOUT THE TEXT

Some might describe the life of Mary as one that was filled with unbearable pain and suffering. To learn that your child's life will be overwhelmed with hate and rejection is incomprehensible for any loving mother. Her experience was at the same time both unique and common. The suffering she experienced is common to all of us. She went through miseries, trials, temptations, and at times panic, such as when she and Joseph sought the young boy, Jesus, for three days before finding Him in the temple (Luke 2:41–49). Yet she is described as having found favor with God (Luke 1:30) because of the work He did in her and for her. From the beginning, God planned for this humble, faithful daughter of the house of David to be the mother of the Christ Child.

God's favor on Mary was twofold: He chose her to be the vessel by which the Word of God was delivered to humankind in the flesh, and He chose her to be the first person to have a personal relationship with the Savior of the world in the flesh and in the Spirit. Mary loved and cared for her Son from the moment He was conceived. She bathed, fed, comforted, encouraged, and prayed for Him. We can assume that as His mother, she delighted in His first words and first steps. We can be sure that she taught Him from the Scriptures and took Him to the temple as a boy, though His understanding far exceeded any mere human understanding. She raised Him with love, a love that was reciprocated with His respect and obedience during His childhood. But along with the events that filled her heart with laughter and joy, she carried the weight of knowing that her child was born to fulfill a divine mission for her heavenly Father. The annunciation (Luke 1:30–33) to Mary symbolizes the start of a new relationship between us and God the Father. Humankind is blessed with His presence among us. This session on Mary's life shows her relationship with Jesus as she surrendered her authority as His earthly mother and received Him as her divine Savior. We as believers are favored because of the work God did through her to keep His promise of a Savior to us.

OUR MENTOR—MARY

Scripture Reading: Matthew 1:18–25; 2:1–15; 12:46–50; 13:53–58; Luke 1:26–56; 2:8–35, 41–52; 4:16–30; 8:20–21; John 2:1–12; 19:17–27

1. During the annunciation, the angel Gabriel greeted Mary by calling her what name that troubled her? See Luke 1:26–38.

    _____

    _____

    _____

    _____

    _____

    _____

2. What does the Bible tell us about the favor of God? See Matthew 6:33; 2 Chronicles 15:2.

    _____

    _____

    _____

    _____

    _____

    _____

3. What is the importance of the words, "The Lord is with you" (Luke 1:28)?

    _____

    _____

    _____

    _____

    _____

    _____

4. What Old Testament verses may have been familiar to Mary that nurtured her faith to trust the Word of God by responding, "Let it be to me according to your word" (Luke 1:38)? See Deuteronomy 31:6; Joshua 1:1–9; Psalm 23; 46:1; 139:7–18; Isaiah 41:10.

_____

_____

_____

_____

_____

5. What New Testament verses can we study to nurture our faith to trust in the Word of God and respond to Him as Mary did, "Let it be to me according to your word" (Luke 1:38) in our life? See John 16:16–24; Romans 4:13–25; 5:1–5; 8:1–11; Philippians 4:11–13; Hebrews 12:1–2.

_____

_____

_____

_____

_____

6. What experiences caused Mary to go to God in prayer for His divine protection and instruction that strengthened her faith in knowing He is ever-present in all circumstances? See Matthew 1:18–19; 2:1–12; 13:53–58; Luke 4:16–30.

_____

_____

_____

_____

_____

7. What experiences would cause Mary to go to God in praise for confirmation of His work of salvation in her life? See Matthew 1:20–25; 2:1–15; Luke 1:39–45; 2:8–19, 22–33; John 2:11.

_____

_____

_____

_____

_____

8. What experiences would cause Mary to go to God in prayer for understanding and acceptance of the changes that were happening in her relationship with Jesus as His mother? See Matthew 12:46–50; Luke 2:34–35, 41–52; 8:20–21; John 2:11.

_____

_____

_____

_____

_____

9. What behavior showed Mary's faith in Jesus' work on earth? See John 2:3–5.

_____

_____

_____

_____

10. What experience did God provide to Mary to show that He was still with her in her darkest time? See John 7:1–6; 19:17–27.

_____

_____

_____

SESSION CONCLUSION

Undoubtedly, Mary was a prayer warrior. Prayer is a powerful gift God has provided us so we can communicate to Him. Throughout most of Mary's life, she prayed directly to our heavenly Father. However, after the crucifixion, she prayed with the others in the Upper Room for Christ's divine guidance in replacing one of the apostles. They prayed, "You, Lord, who know the hearts of all, show which one of these two you have chosen" (Acts1:24). "This is the confidence that we have toward Him, that if we ask anything according to His will He hears us. And if we know that He hears us in whatever we ask, we know that we have the requests that we have asked of Him" (1 John 5:14–15). Her prayers were grounded in her faith and belief in God's will and purpose in her life. As any devoted mother, she would have loved to have seen her Son live in peace and prosperity, but she was submissive to God's will. Just as God responded to the prayers of Mary, Jesus' mother, so our heavenly Father works on our behalf because we inherited the favor of God through our relationship with His Son.

The events in Mary's life point us to Jesus' mission and work for our salvation. In Luke 1:46–55, Mary's song of praise to God, she humbly acknowledged herself as His servant and thanked Him for His remembrance of a deliverer. We must be intentional about maintaining a prayer life with God through Jesus. Yet, our heavenly Father already knows our hearts and prayers, even before we pray. Through Him comes our salvation. "Blessed be the God and Father of our Lord Jesus Christ, who has blessed us in Christ with every spiritual blessing" (Ephesians 1:3). With the help of the Holy Spirit, we believe in Jesus' gift of salvation through faith. After Jesus' ascension in Acts 1:6–11, we see Mary counted among the disciples and others (Acts 1:12–14). They were praying to receive the spiritual guidance of Jesus in choosing an apostle to take the place of Judas. This prayer that they lifted up to Jesus as their heavenly Lord and Savior gives us evidence that our ancient Christian brothers and sisters believed that through Him comes all that we need. God is watching over us and is ready to listen to us right now! We stay committed to God's will through the study of His Word and our relationship with Jesus, in His Holy Supper and by giving Him our thanks and praise in prayer!

PRAYER STARTER

Dear Lord God, thank You for keeping Your promise to send me Jesus Christ, Your beloved Son. Thank You, Lord, for my personal spiritual inheritance of favor because of Your love for me. In Jesus' name and for His sake, I pray. Amen.

PRAYER PROMPTS

1. "Give attention to the sound of my cry, my King and my God, for to You do I pray." (Psalm 5:2)

2. "A person cannot receive even one thing unless it is given him from heaven." (John 3:27)

3. "Do not be anxious about tomorrow, for tomorrow will be anxious for itself. Sufficient for the day is its own trouble." (Matthew 6:34)

STUDY SUMMARY

Christian diligence involves a lifelong struggle to remain in a relationship with God. Just as we do today, the early Christians struggled to keep their faith (Hebrews 11:13–16). They experienced the same inner conflict we do when we try to understand that God is glorified through suffering.

In Hebrews 12:5–11, we learn that God disciplines us because He treats us as His children, just as earthly parents provide boundaries for their children, whom they love. God personalizes His discipline to our individual needs, just as parents do with their own children. We cannot stay obedient to God because we are sinful by nature and because it is hard to see the outcome in the midst of what we are experiencing. Our only chance to live is faith in Jesus as our Savior. As Hebrews 11:1 tells us, "Faith is the assurance of things hoped for, the conviction of things not seen."

The discipline we experience from God throughout our lifetime is the process of spiritual formation. His desire is to make us ready for eternal life through the work of the Holy Spirit in us on earth. The self-discipline we continually strive for in our relationship with God is to be mediated by the External Word and Sacrament, to submit our language, feelings, behavior, and attitude to Christ.

SESSION ANSWER KEYS

SESSION 1 ANSWER KEY: OUR MENTOR—MOSES

Scripture Reading: Numbers 11:4–25

1. God saw the lack of thankfulness among the people. They rejected His heavenly gift of food and praised the foods they enjoyed in Egypt. Their ungratefulness caused Moses to complain about the responsibility of their care to God in prayer.

2. Personal response.

3. God responded to Moses with understanding, and He showed His willingness to help Moses by appointing helpers and giving them the same spiritual gifts as Moses. He also sent quail for the people to eat. However, He showed disappointment and anger toward the people because they were acting rebellious. Their complaining was an expression of ungratefulness for God's choice of their provisions.

4. Moses questioned the amount of meat available from earthly resources: flock and herd, fish from the sea.

5. God responded, "Do you think that I cannot do what I say? Now, watch what will happen" (paraphrased).

6. God responded to Moses out of compassion for him.

SESSION 2 ANSWER KEY: OUR MENTOR—JOSHUA

Scripture Reading: Numbers 11:26–29; 27:18–23; Joshua 1:1–10

1. Two men who had not met in the tent with Moses were prophesying in the camp. Joshua thought the men were doing something wrong and were assuming authority to rise up against Moses.

2. Moses told Joshua that he need not defend his authority from God. Moses was willing to accept any help God offered to him.

3. Moses corrected Joshua's understanding regarding human authority and God's authority.

4. We should not make laws and rules in order to limit one another; this action has no place in God's will.

5. God directed Moses to lay his hand on Joshua and commission him to serve as leader of the Israelites.

6. God promised Joshua that He would never leave him during his lifetime. He told Joshua that the relationship between them would be the same as it was with Moses.

7. Personal response.

SESSION 3 ANSWER KEY: OUR MENTOR—SOLOMON

Scripture Reading: 1 Kings 3:1–15; 9:1–9; 10:1–23; 11:1–10

1. The areas of marriage and governance directly impacted Solomon's relationship with God.

2. Solomon realized the massive scope of his role as king and willingly acknowledged his lack of experience in taking on new responsibilities, especially in regard to making correct decisions for the benefit of the people.

3. Solomon assumed that his purposes were outside the guidance of God. He made a political marriage to a pagan woman as a treaty with the pharaoh. This marriage was in direct violation of God's covenant.

4. The importance of the second appearance is that God saw that Solomon and his sons were getting into spiritual trouble. God reminded Solomon of the covenant that He had made with him and that would be extended to all of his sons if they kept the commandments.

5. God gave Solomon more gold, jewels, and ivory than any other king on earth. He also gave Solomon wisdom to answer any question without regard to its difficulty.

6. Personal response. Discussion may include the long-term or residual effects of circumstances such as parents' divorce or neglect, a teacher's inaction or inability, another relative's life choices or betrayal, and similar situations that have a domino effect on the reader's spiritual and emotional well-being.

7. Solomon cared more about pleasing his wives than pleasing God. Solomon did not heed God's warning regarding marrying foreign women with pagan beliefs. He became involved in idol worship because of his desire to stay at peace with these women, which caused him to turn away from God.

SESSION 4 ANSWER KEY: OUR MENTOR—ESTHER

Scripture Reading: the Book of Esther

1. We see God's preparation begin long before Esther's birth. He placed the unborn, future Queen Esther in the Persian kingdom. The king of Persia removed his wife, Queen Vashti, from the throne and selected Esther to take her place.

2. The plans made by God are from His heart to all generations; all the days of my life were known to Him before I was born. The outcome of plans made by God for me, His baptized and redeemed child, are for my good. Ultimately, God plans for me to spend eternity in heaven with Him.

3. Mordecai recognized that this new role was from God, and he showed his acceptance of it by raising Esther as his daughter, which included teaching her about God.

4. Personal response.

5. Mordecai was thinking about Esther's personal safety. Esther was a captive of war. She had inherited her status as an exile from her homeland.

6. Although Mordecai was a descendant of King Saul, he did not want to jeopardize Esther's position in the Persian king's court. Nevertheless, he was faithful and submissive to God's decree. God knew that Mordecai would publicly respect and obey the Law of God when it came in direct opposition to the law of the king. Mordecai acknowledged God and demonstrated his willingness to be redirected for God's purposes, knowing that he had made himself vulnerable to physical harm.

7. Again, we see God's plan in contrast to human plans. Surely, Mordecai and Esther were not the only Israelites keeping their heritage a secret. Through their grief, God inspired a public protest, causing them to forget about their own plan and focus on prayer and mourning for deliverance. God responded to their grief with His saving grace. The whole kingdom of believers and unbelievers witnessed the faith of the Israelites and the relationship they had with the true God as He delivered them from their enemy.

8. Personal response.

9. God caused Esther to evolve from thinking as an ordinary woman to one who was increasing in a mature spiritual connection. Her awakening was expressed by her words, "If I perish, I perish" (Esther 4:16). Her faith in God motivated her action once she recognized His will and accepted it as the final authority. God gives power and strength to those who feel faint and weak (see Isaiah 40:29).

SESSION 5 ANSWER KEY: OUR MENTOR—PAUL

Scripture Reading: Acts 16:1–40

1. Paul, Silas, and Timothy stopped near the river to pray, and Lydia, a worshiper of God, heard them speaking. God opened her heart to Paul's words. She was led by the Holy Spirit to welcome them into her home, and her whole household was baptized.

2. Personal response.

3. A young slave girl was possessed by a demonic spirit, which gave her the power to tell fortunes for profit to her owners. She followed Paul and Silas around the public place, shouting to everyone that they were servants of God and that they proclaimed the way to salvation.

4. The owners became angry about their loss of profit and wanted revenge against Paul and Silas. Paul and Silas were beaten and put into prison.

5. Paul and Silas intentionally concentrated on the Savior, building up their faith by praying and singing hymns in praise to the Lord. They witnessed to the others in the prison, showing their faith in God's ability to help them. Many events took place that night:

    - The prison doors were opened

    - All prisoners' bonds were unfastened

    - The jailer asked for salvation and Baptism for himself and his family

    - There was rejoicing in the jailer's home for the new believers in God

    - Magistrates wanted to release the prisoners out of fear for their wrongdoing

    - Paul and Silas were released with the magistrates physically present to show public knowledge of their release

    - Paul and Silas received an apology

    - Paul and Silas were asked to leave the city

6. Answers will vary but may include that the dismantling of the prison is symbolic for any circumstances that overwhelm, challenge, or threaten us.

7. The jailer asks, "What must I do to be saved?" They told him, "Believe in the Lord Jesus, and you will be saved" (Acts 16:30–31). The jailer wanted his family to receive the Good News of the Gospel and share in the joy of salvation given freely to all of us by God. They received the message by hearing it from Paul and Silas. They believed and were baptized.

SESSION 6 ANSWER KEY: OUR MENTOR—DAVID

Scripture Reading: 1 Samuel 16:1–17:37

1. God had rejected the current king, Saul, and had sent Samuel to anoint a new king.

2. God told Samuel that His choice was not Eliab. God does not see humankind the same way we do. He does not look at the outward appearance of any person; instead, He looks inward at the person's heart.

3. It was the commitment to God in David's heart. God wanted a king who would not seek false gods but would stay dedicated to Him. In Exodus 20:5, God warned that He is a jealous God and that we should not bow down to or serve any other gods.

4. David responded in faith. He told Eliab that Goliath had no authority to cause fear in God's people (1 Samuel 17:26). He offered himself as a sacrifice for Israel (v. 32).

5. Have confidence in the Lord's salvation, which creates inner peace (Psalm 62:1–2). Trust God in difficult times by continuing to pray in faith (Psalm 63:1). Confess my sins to God so I can be forgiven by Him and freed from developing a prideful heart, which causes me to reject His Holy Word (1 John 1:5–10). Ask God and be patient for an answer (James 1:1–8). Believe that God hears my prayers (1 Peter 3:12). Trust in the guidance that God is giving me and not try to figure things out on my own (Proverbs 3:5–6).

6. David was discounted three times. First, by his father, when he was not called to be present with his brothers for the consecration to make a sacrifice to God (1 Samuel 16:11). Second, by his brother Eliab, when he accused David of arrogance and sarcastically asked, in an effort to demote the task of shepherding and ability of David, "With whom have you left those few sheep in the wilderness?" (1 Samuel 17:28). Finally, by Saul, who compared him to Goliath (1 Samuel 17:33).

7. Personal response.

SESSION 7 ANSWER KEY: OUR MENTOR—ABRAHAM

Scripture Reading: Genesis 12:1–13:4

1. God told Abraham to take his family, leave his pagan homeland, and go to a land that He would show him. In addition, God said that He would make Abraham a great name and nation. God told Abraham exactly what His purpose was for his life.

2. God caused Abraham to recognize his sin of worshiping idols and allowed him to be ministered to in the Word. When God spoke directly to Abraham, His Word caused faith and opened his heart, and he believed.

3. Abraham left Haran and took his wife, his nephew Lot, their possessions, and the people he had acquired in Haran and traveled until the Lord came to him again. Abraham built an altar to God because he heard, believed, and trusted His Word.

4. Personal response.

5. God was teaching Abraham to be obedient to Him. Abraham experienced extreme vulnerability and suffering at the hands of those he sought to trust. Through these experiences, God was increasing Abraham's faith to know that God is real and to be content with His gifts.

6. The trials I face will require me to mature in faith, producing patience to trust God and not be anxious. When I feel afraid, I will focus my thoughts through prayer and study of His Word, building my trust in God.

7. Abraham returned to the land, set up his tent, built an altar to God, and made a sacrifice on it. At the altar, Abraham praised God for his rescue.

8. The outcome of God's plan is always good for me. God's plan is perfectly complete. He knows the past, present, and future.

SESSION 8 ANSWER KEY: OUR MENTOR—JOB

Scripture Reading: Job 1–2; 42

1. God reprimanded Jonah regarding his anger toward God for granting favor to people he believed were undeserving of it (Jonah 3:6–4:11). God granted favor to Abel and not to Cain, although both made an offering to Him. One was made with the expectation to influence God, while the other was made in true faith (see Genesis 4:3–7). God grants favor to those who are obedient to His will (Luke 1:28–30).

2. God grants favor as a protector of those who stay faithful to Him (see Daniel 1:8–17). God granted favor to Enoch because of his faithfulness (Hebrews 11:5). God was pleased with David's desire to build Him a dwelling place (Acts 7:44–46). God grants favor for ministerial work by increasing faith and church membership (see Acts 2:42–47). God grants favor and is pleased with spiritual maturity and growth (Luke 2:46–52).

3. Job was concerned for his children and offered sacrifices in an effort to gain God's forgiveness for each sinful and corrupt behavior committed by his family.

4. Job maintained his faith in God, saying, "The LORD gave, and the LORD has taken away; blessed be the name of the LORD" (Job 1:21).

5. Job's wife encouraged him to curse God and die.

6. Job's friends were filled with emotion, expressing signs of grief: screaming and crying, tearing clothes, and sprinkling dust. Afterward, they became silent for seven days and nights. A large portion of the Book of Job depicts his three friends as they attempted to comprehend his circumstances, with each showing how his own human reasoning was limited. Job submitted to his own lack of understanding, in concert with realizing that God is in control.

7. God puts us in difficult situations, as He did Job. God led Job through experiences that forced him to confess, repent, and desire a closer relationship with Him. Job believed that he was earning God's favor through his behavior. In other words, he thought he could save himself. He learned that he had no bargaining power with God.

8. The Lord restored Job, providing him with more than he had before.

9. Personal response.

SESSION 9 ANSWER KEY: OUR MENTOR—MARY

Scripture Reading: Matthew 1:18–25; 2:1–15; 12:46–50; 13:53–58; Luke 1:26–56; 2:8–35, 41–52; 4:16–30; 8:20–21; John 2:1–12; 19:17–27

1. The angel Gabriel spoke to Mary, "O favored one, the Lord is with you!" (Luke 1:29).

2. God seeks those who desire to please Him more than themselves or others.

3. Mary had a strong faith, humble heart, and desire to please the Lord. The Lord was with her at that very moment and would be with her through the duration of fulfilling His work in her and for her.

4. Response to biblical verses.

5. Response to biblical verses.

6. Joseph considered divorce in response to Mary's pregnancy. King Herod tried to kill the Christ Child. Jesus returned home to public rejection in Nazareth. Jesus was threatened with stoning in Nazareth.

7. Joseph had faith and believed in the miracle birth. Shepherds heard of Christ's birth and believed. Wise Men believed and sought the Christ Child. Elizabeth believed, and the unborn John the Baptist acknowledged the presence of the Savior. God's promise of His Word in the flesh was nurtured in Mary's womb. Simeon and Anna believed and praised God during the dedication of the Christ Child. Disciples believed at the wedding in Cana.

8. Simeon's words regarding Mary's pain paralleled those Christ experienced on the cross. Mary and twelve-year-old Jesus interacted at the temple. Spiritual believers are prioritized over earthly family. Jesus taught that our family of flesh is temporary, while the family of God is eternal.

9. Mary looked to Jesus to care for others. She asked in faith for His help to provide the wine that was needed at the wedding.

10. Jesus presented Mary to John in a mother-son relationship at the foot of the cross. God did not leave her in the care of unbelievers.

READING GROUP DISCUSSION GUIDE

SESSION 1 GROUP DISCUSSION QUESTIONS: MOSES

1. Why do you think Moses questioned God about from where the food would come?

    Discussion should consider that Moses was thinking about provisions from nature, not from God.

2. What do you think God meant when He said to the people, "You have rejected the LORD who is among you" (Numbers 11:20)?

    Discussion should consider that God has been with the people, caring for them and protecting them. They have experienced God in a real personal way, and they chose to dismiss or ignore His presence in their lives.

3. What was the difference between the people's attitude and Moses' attitude toward God in their complaining?

    Discussion should consider that Moses was weary and frustrated as he worked to fulfill God's work. The people were grumbling while expressing an attitude of entitlement, acting as if God owed them His blessings.

4. How do you feel about God's ability to provide for your needs, based on what He said to Moses in Numbers 11:23?

SESSION 2 GROUP DISCUSSION QUESTIONS: JOSHUA

1. Explain how Joshua was accountable to God.

    Discussion should consider Joshua 1:6–9: Joshua should study God's Word, have faith that God is with him, believe that his strength came from God, and strive to be successful in God's eyes, not in the eyes of the world.

2. How should we respond today to the message God gave to Joshua?

    Discussion should consider that we cannot serve God without studying His Scripture. Without God, we are weak, helpless, and lost.

SESSION 3 GROUP DISCUSSION QUESTIONS: SOLOMON

1. What should Solomon's authority have been over his household? See Joshua 24:15; Colossians 2:16–23.

   Discussion should consider Solomon's commitment to his covenant with God; his profession of faith should not have altered. Compare his behavior with Joshua's statement, "But as for me and my house, we will serve the LORD" (Joshua 24:15). Christianity will never be replaced by human religions (Colossians 2:16–23).

2. How does the message in 1 Kings 9:1–9 apply to us today?

   Discussion should consider that Solomon had many marriages. These were not marriages that conformed to God's teachings for the Israelites. Solomon may have been driven by desire of power and lust, as well as pompousness (enjoying the position of king too much), and developed a sense of entitlement.

3. What was revealed as God's truth among the members of Solomon's vast family? See 1 Kings 11:1–6; Deuteronomy 7:3–4; 23:3–6.

   Discussion should consider how Solomon married women from six different regions with six different beliefs for worshiping pagan gods. These women taught their beliefs to their children, influenced Solomon to build temples for their gods so they could worship them, and caused disruption because of their beliefs in both the family (his sons) and the Israelite community.

SESSION 4 GROUP DISCUSSION QUESTIONS: ESTHER

1. Why does obedience to God cause us to feel vulnerable? See Isaiah 55:8–9.

   Discussion should consider that we hear in Isaiah that our thoughts and ways are not the thoughts and ways of the Lord. With this understanding, it is normal for us to feel vulnerable when we recognize God's will and are obedient to it. However, our relationship with God makes us brave as we study His Word, giving us strong faith to be obedient.

2. Explain how God takes time to establish His will in our lives, using the timeline of Esther's life as an example. See Esther 2:1–8.

   Discussion should consider that God is the creator of time and is not bound by its limitations. Esther was a descendant of Kish, a Benjamite who had been captured, exiled from the homeland, and brought into Susa the citadel (a city outside of the actual kingdom) by Nebuchadnezzar, the king of Babylon, generations before her birth.

3. How would you explain the relationship between God and Mordecai when God rearranged Mordecai's plan for secrecy, forcing him to admit to his faith and heritage? See Matthew 10:32–39.

   Discussion should consider that the relationship between God and Mordecai was strong. God knew that Mordecai's faith was strong enough to trust Him as he exposed himself to death for the sake of acknowledging his faith. As a part of God's divine plan, this was the exact moment He had planned for Mordecai to claim Him as the ultimate authority over his life.

4. How does God prepare us to recognize and accept His Word as final authority and be obedient to it? See Hebrews 5:1–10; Acts 10:9–48.

   Discussion should consider how God prepares us for obedience through our experiences. During personal challenges, He ministers to us. Jesus offered prayers with cries and tears to God and was heard. Though He was God the Son, He demonstrated obedience in the things He suffered (Hebrews 5:7–10). In another example, the Lord prepared Peter to establish the first Gentile church mission by sending him a vision that showed His approval for Peter to eat foods that were against the Jewish laws. The voice of God told Peter that God Himself had cleansed the food; therefore, Peter could go without hesitation to the Gentiles to establish God's Church (Acts 10:9–48).

5. What do we understand about the struggle to stay obedient to God no matter the circumstances or challenges? See Hebrews 12:1–11.

Discussion should consider that the early Christians struggled with confessing Christ and keeping His statutes, and so will we. It is undeniable that we will continue to sin while striving to be holy; however, through the struggle we are prepared for eternal life. We believe in the promises of God and are willing to be corrected by Him. In addition, we understand that discipline can be filled with sorrow, but believers trained by God's discipline prove their discipleship because His discipline is good for us.

SESSION 5 GROUP DISCUSSION QUESTIONS: PAUL

1. What was the difference in the responses of Lydia and the slave girl toward Paul?

   Discussion should consider how Lydia responded in faith to God, opening her heart to receive His message (Acts 16:14–15). The demon possessing the girl recognized God's presence and was driven to respond (see also Luke 4:34–41).

2. Why do you think Paul and Silas stayed silent for days in response to the demon's behavior toward them?

   Discussion should consider that Scripture does not tell us exactly. But let's put ourselves in this situation. When we have been annoyed by someone over a period of time, what might be our first response? Perhaps we would ignore them, thinking that they would eventually go away on their own. Possibly, Paul was refraining from acting zealously, as was his natural inclination, and choosing to practice self-discipline by taking time for prayer and deep meditation as to how best to respond. In the days of silence, Paul may have been praying for God to show him the appropriate time and action to handle the problem.

3. What was the importance of silencing what the demon was saying about Paul and the others in the marketplace? See Acts 16:17.

Discussion should consider that the importance of stopping the demon was to assure that no one associated it with God. The demon was driven to acknowledge God's presence and draw attention to His gift of salvation; it was not a response of faith.

SESSION 6 GROUP DISCUSSION QUESTIONS: DAVID

1. What was the importance of David's time in the mountains that caused him to develop such an intimate relationship with God? See 1 Samuel 17:34–37.

   Discussion should consider that during the time in the mountains, God produced faith in David through experiences that committed David to God. David developed a dependency on God that resulted in him becoming obedient to His instruction without hesitation. David became convicted in his belief that God is real.

2. How might you compare David's time in the mountains to Jesus' time in the wilderness?

   Discussion should consider that both David and Jesus were removed from other people. They became totally dependent upon God for everything. They talked with God, but more importantly, they spent a lot of time listening to Him. The wilderness provided a sanctuary for them to be ministered to by God.

SESSION 7 GROUP DISCUSSION QUESTIONS: ABRAHAM

1. Compare the narrative of Abraham leaving the land promised to him by God with that of James 5:19–20.

   Discussion should consider the text in James: "If anyone among you wanders from the truth and someone brings him back, . . . whoever brings back a sinner from his wandering will save his soul from death and will cover a multitude of sins." Abraham was brought back to the land given to him by God. God restored him through his confession and the sacrifice he made at the altar.

2. As Abraham (Abram) explored the land, what caused him to react as an ordinary man, resulting in abandoning God's plan? See Genesis 12:10–20.

    Discussion should consider that Abraham (Abram) saw that there was a famine in the land. He took it upon himself to move out of the land and closer to Egypt, thinking to get near what seemed like better land. He had given no thought to God. He had not gone to God to inquire or ask for a confirmation of this move. Encourage the group to expand on this decision in terms of our behavior. We receive God's blessings and use them or don't, as we see fit.

SESSION 8 GROUP DISCUSSION QUESTIONS: JOB

1. How would you explain the implications of Job's wife encouraging him to curse God and die? See Romans 5:1–5.

    Discussion should consider that suicide would be the implication. Nowadays, many doctors and family members encourage people to escape from the suffering and pain experienced in life by committing medically assisted suicide. However, if we allow God to use our bodies as living sacrifices for the sake of ourselves and others, then we must have faith that our suffering is for His glory and our good.

2. Explain how the restoration that God worked in Job's life proves to us that God uses hardships to gain our attention and change our heart and attitude. See Job 42:10–13.

    Discussion should consider that God helped Job understand that His work is done through the Holy Spirit. God caused Job to repent of his attitude in confronting God with justifications for why he should possess a certain quality of life. Job recognized that his attitude needed to change toward God, and he felt sincere remorse once he understood that his attitude toward God was wrong. Job repented and asked God to forgive his friends, because they did not understand the work God was doing to develop his character into a mature man of faith. God accepted Job's prayer of forgiveness for his friends and returned him to a close relationship with Himself.

3. What was missing from Job's life as a believer before these experiences? See Job 42:5.

    Discussion should consider that Job was missing a personal relationship with God. After these events, Job had a personal story to share with others about God. He had a true testimony to share about God's mercy and grace. Through his experience, Job modeled for us how necessary it is to have our very own, very real, personal relationship with God. Job's experience provides us with a deeper understanding of our personal relationship with God, both in good times and bad. We also are submissive to God's will in our lives, regardless of our circumstances, and focus on His blessings and mercy during every experience of our lives.

SESSION 9 GROUP DISCUSSION QUESTIONS: MARY

1. Why do you think the description "O favored one" (Luke 1:28) was troubling for Mary?

    Discussion should consider that Mary understood that being favored by God meant that God was calling on someone for a special role. Mary had been taught about God's relationship with some of the favored people from the Old Testament, such as Moses, David, Noah, Abraham, and Daniel. She understood the seriousness of His favor from their experiences. She perceived herself as a humble servant and could not with her own understanding realize why God had chosen her.

2. Why was God's favor on Mary so important to her life?

    Discussion should consider that God's favor was the spiritual strength that she would need to be the dedicated and supportive mother of the Christ Child as He matured. God created in her a strong commitment to believe in His promise through study of His Holy Word so that she could meditate and lean on it during various times throughout her life. God's favor allowed her to pray for and recognize His mercy, grace, and endurance operating in her daily life.

3. Why is it important to understand what God calls favor in our lives as believers?

    Discussion should consider that it is important to understand how God perceives favor in our lives because it helps us to live according to His will. He provides His favor to make us ready to receive His gift of eternal salvation.

A CONVERSATION WITH MARGO

Why did you write Be Thou My Guide?

This study stems from my personal effort to seek a deeper understanding of who God is and how I could be sure that I was living my life aligned to His plan. I really wanted to know Him. About twenty-five years ago, I met Julie, an intern whom I selected to work in my training office and who later became a dear friend. She was a gift from God. As our friendship developed, I learned to admire her relationship with God. As she shared about her relationship with God, I felt myself awaken spiritually in ways that I could never have imagined. The Lord brought Julie into my life because He knew it was time for me to mature as a Christian. I believe that I was ready to allow the Lord to work in my life because I truly believed in Him and prayed to Him; however, I had not been ready to hear God speak to me.

Why did you provide a section in each session called "Relational Understanding"?

I believe a narrative about each objective is an important component for those who may have difficulty with making a personal connection to the faith relationships between God and the biblical people. In addition, I sometimes hear it said that people are too relational. I find that interesting, when it is exactly how God made us. God wants a relationship with us, and we should take full advantage of that understanding to help others connect to Him.

What do you mean by relational understanding?

Each one of us is called to have our very own relationship with God. That is what God wants us to understand about Him and seek from Him. It is very important to find ways to help one another get to the deepest level of belief in God as a real presence in our lives. As we grow in our faith, we must be clear that it is God doing the increasing in us. We must stay clear of self-imposed religious practices and traditions that don't help with developing a relationship to God. In his Letter to the Colossians, the apostle Paul explained the importance of helping one another stay rooted in the true teaching of Jesus. He encouraged the Colossians to help one another: "See to it that no one takes you captive by philosophy and empty deceit, according to human tradition, according to the elemental spirits of the world, and not according to Christ. For in Him the whole fullness of deity dwells bodily" (Colossians 2:8–9). Paul's message to us is all that we need to know about God the Father, as revealed to us in Christ. We can help one another to understand that what God offers is real, true, and relevant to current life.

Were you raised in a Christian home?

Yes, I was. My family was very involved in church life. As a high school and college student, I served as a choir member, usher, and lay reader. There are many generations of pastors and church workers at all levels in the church. My father's family was Baptist, and my mother was raised as a Methodist. However, I believe that God calls us to mature at different times in our lives, and He sent Julie to me for the next level of my maturity as a wife and mother at that time.

Was there a specific time when you remember God calling you to mature as a wife and mother?

Yes, it was the summer of 1997. Brian and I took our family to Bair Lake Camp. Julie had extended the invitation, and I knew that we needed this time together away in order to hear in what direction God wanted us to move with respect to our marriage, our family, and our individual selves. That summer, we studied the Christian roles of husband, wife, parents, children, and the overall Christian lifestyle. We knew that we wanted to be together as a family, but we were still struggling with how to make it work. Our inherited tools from childhood, young adulthood, and first marriages had not provided the type of support for what we wanted in our lives as a couple, although we were raised in families with mothers who believed in the Lord.

Was there anything else that you wanted to share?

In 1998, we returned to Bair Lake for another family camp and Bible study. That summer, we studied how to pray to God. Once back home, I made a deliberate decision to try to hear the Lord speaking to me. I made some efforts to study the Bible through group study with a cell group; I focused on making time to study the Bible on my own as well. I worked at changing the focus of my prayers by not always telling God what my problems were but by focusing on praising the Lord for His own sake and thanking Him for being with me at all times. I began to seek the Lord's guidance in every situation by reviewing my Bible at every opportunity; I slowed my pace of mind and physical activity in order to allow the Word to grasp my attention. I shared my new way of thinking with my children and husband; we worked at tithing as a deliberate act. Brian and I began to spend time together in prayer. As our children grew older, they became active in church work. My son was a youth crucifer and acolyte. Our daughters sang in the youth choir.

In 1999, Brian had become active as president of the men's group at church. He was very involved and set up a yearly men's retreat program. I supported his service to the church. During this time, Brian was approached by the ministers of the church district as a possible candidate for the ministry. Brian believed that he was not yet ready for the commitment but felt it was a calling that he might accept at a later time in his life.

Also during the year of 1999, we joined a group of married couples in the church to organize a couple's ministry. We got a lot of joy out of our involvement with this group. We studied from the *Couples' Devotional Bible* on a weekly basis. We learned a lot about the way the Lord wanted us to function as a Christian couple and how to keep the Lord our focus in our marriage. We came to understand that God is the head of our marriage and that our marriage is a Christian pilgrimage.

In 2000, I decided that I could devote some of my personal time to assisting in the church as an independent unit instead of as a support unit to choices of service that my children and husband were making in the church. I joined the altar guild and volunteered to assist as an announcer of church activities. I really did enjoy being of service. I also enjoyed learning to do something new in the church that I had not done as a young person growing up in the church. In concert, Brian worked as an elder in the church and served on a committee to develop communication with a church in the Ann Arbor area, focusing on discussing race relations with a church in Detroit. He also was a founding member of the Urban Church Men's Association. This group of men derived from various Lutheran churches in the metro area.

Would you say God was preparing you and your husband for more?

Looking back, I can definitely follow God's guidance and direction in our lives and in our marriage. I can now see how God prepared us and opened our hearts and mind to recognize and accomplish His will for our lives.

What do you find most curious about your life so far?

I find most curious how God began to prepare me for serving with my husband in the ministry through sending a student intern into my life. I thought it was my responsibility to simply prepare her for the next journey of her career after graduate school; instead, God sent her to help prepare us for a faith journey that we could never have imagined.